A Presidency Under Pressure
The Media's Portrayal of President Trump's Election and First 100 Days

Jake Eberlein, M.A.

MEDIATRIX PRESS

MMXVII

A Presidency under Pressure

ISBN-13: 978-0692899342
ISBN-10: 0692899340

1st Edition

© Jacob Eberlein, 2017
All Rights Reserved. No portion of this may be reproduced in electronic or physical format without the express permission of the publisher.

Mediatrix Press
607 E. 6th Ave, Ste. 230
Post Falls, ID 83854
http://www.mediatrixpress.com

TABLE OF CONTENTS

PREFACE. v

Part I – The Election

Chapter I
      Donald Trumps Clinton. 1

Chapter II
      Not My President. 9

Chapter III
      The Billion Dollar Cabinet. 17

Chapter IV
      The Recount. 27

Chapter V
      From Russia With Love. 35

Chapter VI
      You Are Fake News. 45

Part II – The First 100 Days

Chapter VII
      Make America Great Again. 55

Chapter VIII
    Keeping the Bad Dudes Out.. 61

Chapter IX
    Address to the Nation.. 69

Chapter X
    Trials and Errors. 77

Chapter XI
    Go Nuclear.. 85

Chapter XII
    Tweet the Truth. 93

Notes. 101

Preface

This work is the result of simply checking the news every day. Millions of Americans do just that before starting the workday, while taking a break during the day, while relaxing in the evening, or while engaging in a host of other activities. The media is a pastime for many of us, and for better or worse, people get their vital information from the media. Is it fact, truth, or fake? Unfortunately, that is often left up to the reader to decide. Despite that point, there are many excellent options out there to gather the daily news.

I first got the idea to write a book portraying the US presidency through the eyes of the media during the final year of the Obama administration. Then, as I watched the news coverage leading up to the presidential election runoff between Hillary Clinton and Donald Trump the possibility of starting the project with the winner of that election materialized. So much was going on in the media, and when Trump actually won, it became clear that the potential for conflict between the media and the president-elect was already there. Therefore, I decided to take on the role of writing the history of the Trump presidency as portrayed in the media.

Not everything one reads in the news happened just as it is portrayed. That I realize. However, I have not intended to write anything in this book that was not portrayed in the media, and for that matter I have primarily relied on the major news organizations we know, such as CNN, NBC, MSNBC, FOX, The New York Times, The Washington Post, ABC, BBC, CBS, NPR, and USA Today. I have cited a few articles from smaller organizations and only rarely cited

Preface

a fringe news source if it was necessary to get another angle to the story.

   Obviously, this is an incomplete history of the Trump administration since the media is not privy to all of the facts. The complete story of this presidency will be written years from now, when hindsight clarifies the past, and when personal, classified, and otherwise obscure information finally becomes public knowledge. During the course of events today, especially as we perceive them through the media, it is impossible to take down all that actually happened. Furthermore, and as previously mentioned, often the details get misquoted, blurred, and mixed up by the press. So, clearly there may very well be mistakes in this book, though unintentional on the author's part. Nevertheless, they will be left intact since my intent is to write the history of the Trump presidency as we remember it through the lens of the media we view from day to day. Finally, this book neither approves nor disapproves the Trump presidency. It simply gathers diverse information and relays to the reader the events as they unfolded.

Part I – The Election

CHAPTER I
Donald Trumps Clinton

IT was a shocking experience for most Americans. They were sad, angry, crying, and screaming. They were jubilant, celebrating, shouting, and crying with joy. They were gloomy or relieved. The surprise affected them in various ways. Those who supported Hillary Clinton for president of the United States could not, almost would not, believe their senses. On election day, the New York Times gave her an 85% chance of winning the presidential election. But now, she was beginning to lose. For those who supported Donald Trump for president, it was almost too good to be true, but there it was – he was creeping ahead in electoral votes. It was election day, and by about 8 pm on November 8, 2016, Trump supporters became excited. The impossible seemed suddenly possible. As the evening unfolded he continued to make amazing advances. Clinton's supporters remained hopeful until about 10:30 when Trump took Ohio. Then the battle escalated.

News reporters tried to explain how she could still win, yet the attempts were futile. Trump took North Carolina, a battleground state, but Clinton could still win Pennsylvania, Michigan and Wisconsin. Yet, by 11:00 it was obvious that Trump had won, although the media would not admit it. For example, NBC's Chuck Todd tried to belittle the change saying, only "one major news organization" had called the

Presidency Under Pressure

election, yet it was not good enough for NBC and for other news sources. Likewise, it was not good enough for Democrats. Clinton's campaign manager, John Podesta, said at 11:05 that they would not accept the results until all the votes were counted. Clinton disappointed her supporters by not speaking to them that night and they went home. Trump supporters on the other hand, cheered as they waited for Trump to speak to them. It was the Associated Press that first called the race at 11:31 pm – "Donald Trump is elected president of the United States of America."[1] Other organizations followed suit as the night went on.

Clinton called Trump and conceded the election just before midnight, and the president-elect went on stage with his choice for vice-president, Mike Pence, to speak to the American people. "This is a historic night," Pence exclaimed from the stage in Manhattan as he introduced the president-elect. With his family standing nearby, Trump graciously accepted the nomination as president. His victory speech began with gratitude towards Hillary Clinton for her service to America and a call to those from all points of the political spectrum to unite and "bind the wounds of division." He called for everyone to support him to build up the nation and recreate the American Dream. His focus was the people of the United States and what he could do for them. His promises seemed noble – he promised to be fair to everyone. Trump thanked all of those who helped him reach his goal. For his supporters, it was a dream come true. It was their moment. The president-elect promised to not let them down.[2]

In the few days before election day there were so many controversies swirling around both candidates. Trump faced allegations of sexual misconduct and fraud. Clinton was still being attacked for deleting her emails and was called a liar on multiple points. Who would win seemed a no brainer – Clinton of course. Yet obviously, Trump had support from the majority of states, and that was what mattered in the presidential election since the electoral college selected the president based on votes within their state. Nonetheless, there was a great deal of negative news about Mr. Trump. He was criticized for not believing intel that Russia had supported hacking that interfered with the US elections. President Obama told the working class not to be "bamboozled" by him and that the real-estate mogul had actually mistreated workers all of his life. Obama urged men to get over sexism and vote for the first woman president. On Halloween Obama told a "spooky" story on television, "Donald Trump could be president."[3]

In fact, those pre-election days belonged to Hillary. Betting in the UK had her in the lead. You had to spend $300 to win $100 tin a bet that she would win. Donald on the other hand? You could bet $100 and win $275.[4] The odds were definitely against Trump. She seemed to have all the support necessary to win. Yet, only 11 days before elections, FBI Director James Comey brought the ultimate October surprise: the reopening of the FBI's investigation into Hillary's emails. The whole thing was oddly connected with another FBI investigation into congressman Anthony Weiner's lewd advances towards a minor. The latter's estranged wife, Huma Abedin, was Clinton's advisor. The FBI said that they found Abedin's emails on Weiner's laptop that had possibly gone through Clinton's server.

Presidency Under Pressure

The Clinton server scandal was all over the media during the election season and the subject wearied both Democrats and Republicans. Reopening the case likely harmed Clinton's candidacy, although it would be difficult to provide statistical evidence to prove it. Nevertheless, Bill Clinton blamed it for Hillary's loss. Trump praised it, saying "thank you Huma." The media commented that it was "beyond precedent" and it was being handled "out of the ordinary." It was certainly shocking to have a presidential candidate under FBI investigation right before elections.[5] It must have surprised Hillary as well, since she was already a week into planning her victory with a spectacular fireworks display.[6]

If Hillary had problems prior to election, Trump had them too. For one thing, he had difficulty uniting the Republican party. Ohio Governor John Kasich, who had run against Trump in the primaries, disliked both Clinton and Trump, so he voted for John McCain. Colin Powell said he would vote for Clinton. The media also reported on likes and dislikes of Europeans. The Italians, for example, seemed to favor Trump, comparing him with their similarly self-made man and down to earth spoken former prime minister, Berlusconi Americano. They did not, however, like Hillary Clinton as she was too much of an insider. Over in Russia, Trump had the support of President Vladimir Putin (this would soon become a serious issue). Back in America, even support caused controversy for Trump when *The Crusader*, the official Ku Klux Klan organ, voiced its support for Trump. Donald's support often seemed to be from the wrong places. One thing was for certain, he did not have support of celebrities, as the media reported, at least 18 claimed they would leave the country if he were elected. Among these were Barbra Streisand, Miley Cyrus, Cher, and Samuel Jackson. They supported Clinton, and she apparently had popular support. For example, she had endorsements from 57 of the Nation's largest newspapers, while Trump only had 2 such endorsements (for Trump this was a record low for any major party candidate).[7]

Speaking of newspapers, Trump made the news media nervous with his name calling. He did not shy from calling the media dishonest, lying, and scum. There was justified concern over their future relationship if Trump won the election. "Journalists worry a lot about precedent because their access isn't inscribed by law but hashed out through arrangements with the White House." Yes, the First Amendment was inscribed in law, but not their relationship with government. "There's nothing stopping Trump from deciding not to hold a daily press briefing or kicking media outlets off the White House grounds. His fans would likely love it," lamented the Huffington Post.[8]

In fact, prior to the election there was a trove of speculative articles wondering what a Trump presidency would be like, and most of it was terrifying. Social activist Michael Moore said that if elected, Trump would be the last president of the United States and would signal the end of the country.[9] One of Trump's neighbors said, "I would be scared to death to see him as our president."[10] Rolling Stone Magazine believed Trump would be Trump as he always was and would be a sexist, lying, bragging, insulting, racist, unqualified, "corrupt manchild who celebrates everything that's ugly about America and not a single thing that's great about it" – in a few words, "Donald Trump cannot be president of the United States."[11] Three Nobel Peace Laureates authored a piece for the Huffington Post, warning the dire consequences to peace if Trump were elected.[12] The Washington Post said that Donald was the "most unpopular nominee in modern history," yet he could still win because Hillary Clinton was also unpopular.[13] In fact, out of 13 important characteristics for the presidency, Trump only led in one: the economy. Yet, that could swing things too. Overall, the media reported the negative features of Trump's bid for office and seemed to neglect the positive aspects which his supporters saw in him. Perhaps that was because the latter's positive vision was a negative thing for the media which tended to support liberal policies. Altogether, the media presented a Trump presidency as filled with war. The Washington Post advised people to hoard imported goods and to get to know alternative news reporters (because the main organs would be discredited by Trump), among other things if Trump won.[14]

Many people after the election said that Comey's FBI investigation did not have an effect on the election and that Trump would have won anyway. While that may be true, it is difficult to prove. On the other hand, Trump did move up in the polls immediately following its reopening. For the first time since May, just one week before the election, he came ahead of Clinton at 46%-45% in the ABC News/Washington Post poll. Other newspapers put him behind, yet it seemed apparent that there was an effect. Nevertheless, within two days, the New York Times/CBS poll put Hillary ahead at 45%-42%. It was certainly a bitter rivalry. With the media, Trump had little support. Melania, his wife, "seeking to soften her husband's coarse image" spoke on the campaign trail for him. As portrayed in the media, it also seemed like he had little public support. Even President Obama promoted Clinton on the campaign trail and pushed very hard against a Trump presidency. On the other hand, Trump's former rival, Marco Rubio, supported him now. For that matter, Hillary's former rival Bernie Sanders now supported her too.[15]

Appearances, however, are not everything and elections are always up in the air until election day. Who could say what would happen. Despite the news chatter, Donald had a message that resonated with voters. He promised to bring jobs back to America, to make America first in policy, to bring wealth back to America, to help the working American to bring down the national debt, to bring back the American Dream, to *make America great again*. He did largely finance his own campaign so that he could be free from owing anyone anything. This helped to drive down the overall campaign cost from $2.76 billion in 2016, to $2.65 billion in 2017.[16] But would Donald be good for the economy? The media said no. Instead, it said that Clinton would perhaps bring the stock market up 10%, but with Trump there would be volatility whatever that was supposed to mean: "market participants expect a stronger economy under Clinton and more risk under Trump."[17]

Against all odds, on November 8, 2016, Donald Trump won the election, taking 304 electoral votes to Hillary's 227 votes. This stunned Clinton supporters nationwide, or perhaps one should say worldwide. Democrats were dumfounded. Michelle Obama said later that she did not even stay up that night to watch the outcome. Instead, she

PRESIDENCY UNDER PRESSURE

went to bed.[18] Bill Clinton afterwards recalled, "at the end, we had the Russians, and the F.B.I. deal, she couldn't prevail against that...But she did everything else. And still won by 2.8 million votes."[19] While her supporters spoke about how she won the popular vote; she did so several million votes behind President Obama's win in 2012. Yet, if she had taken just over 50,000 votes in Michigan, Wisconsin, and Pennsylvania, she could have won the electoral votes there and thus the victory. There was a lot of soul searching. How did Hillary Clinton loose? During the months leading up to elections, the Clinton campaign more and more pointed fingers at Russia for interfering in the US election process. They claimed that the foreign country favored Trump.

Despite the chatter, President-elect Trump met President Obama at the Oval Office on November 10, and the press published a picture of the two shaking hands. Trump said it was an "honor" to meet the president and the two had a 90-minute discussion. Over the next few weeks, Trump would also be briefed on the nation's most secret information, including covert operations and nuclear weapon use.[20] The newly elected president began planning his first actions as president and would especially begin working on improving the economy. Trump, however, was not president yet, and Obama reminded him about this before leaving to visit Greece, Germany and Peru, saying, "there is one president at a time." Obama was proud of his contributions to the nation and elaborated on his success in healthcare, job growth, income increase, and the economy: "America's in the strongest position possible and hopefully there's an opportunity for the next president to build on that."[21]

CHAPTER II
Not My President

CBS interviewed President-elect Trump in *60 Minutes* to find out more about his ideas. While he did not give a whole lot of details, Trump said there was a great deal of work to do and that he did not envision much vacation time. He also pledged to not accept the $400,000 salary of president. The media then debated whether he would even move from his opulent Trump Tower in New York to live at the White House, or if his wife Melania would also move with their son Barron.[1] The newly elected president did not yet disclose any goals or policy agenda, but the media quickly began delving into his previous speeches and announcements to find some. They did find his key promises for his first 100 days. Trump's promise to enforce laws against illegal immigration as well as to defund sanctuary cities immediately alarmed civil rights groups. Other groups were excited about Trump's ability to have a positive impact on the economy. For an updated outline of the 100 days they had to wait until November 21.[2]

Meanwhile, Clinton supporters were constantly looking for ways that Hillary could have won and perhaps could still win. They rioted and complained. Following Election Day, there were anti-Trump protests for weeks, with thousands hoping their actions might change things. They chanted "not my president."[3] Trump's reaction and first tweet after

Presidency Under Pressure

winning the election came on November 11: "Just had a very open and successful presidential election. Now professional protesters, incited by the media, are protesting. Very unfair!" The next morning he tweeted a follow-up, "Love the fact that the small groups of protesters last night have passion for our great country. We will all come together and be proud!"[4] One November 11 rally turned into a "riot" with over 4,000 participating. Obama indirectly supported them, although carefully wording his support, simply stating "I wouldn't advise them to be silent."[5] The protests continued for days upon days following the election as tens of thousands took to the streets in cities across the nation, but they could not change the outcome. Others chimed in that the Electoral College should be abolished, especially since this was the second time that a Democratic candidate had won the popular vote but lost the electoral college. The previous time was when Al Gore lost to Bush in 2000.[6]

Amid the controversy, New Jersey governor Chris Christie, who had been on the victory stage with Trump on November 8, now fell from favor. The governor's legal woes seemed to press hard on his relationship with Trump. Therefore, Mike Pence replaced Christie as head of the presidential transition team on November 11. Other members of the team included Ben Carson, who had run against Trump in the Primaries, former New York City mayor Rudy Giuliani, and Alabama senator Jeff Sessions. This group and a few others, along with Trump's children, Eric, Donald, and Ivanka, and Jared Kushner, his son-in-law, began forming the foundations of the future Trump presidency.[7] The appointment of Pence to head the team was indicative of Trump's growing trust in him. In fact, Pence was an important part of the Trump team. In Pence's own words, he was "a Christian, a conservative and a Republican, in that order." The media commented that Pence brought confidence to the group of conservatives who voted for Trump (who was viewed by many as leaning towards liberal ideas).[8]

If the United States was in transition, the whole world was too. ABC News wrote a story citing some of the "world's most authoritarian leaders" and their support of Donald Trump. Among them were Syrian President Bashar al-Assad, Russian President Vladimir Putin, Philippine President Rodrigo Duterte, Turkish President Recep Tayyip Erdogan, and North Korea's Kim Jong-un. While the latter never commented on the election, he was put into the article as if he supported Trump. Just over a week after the election, Japanese Prime Minister Shinzo Abe visited Trump Tower to meet the new president-elect.[9] The media really made a lot of Putin's support for Trump during the post-election time. Did the Russian president interfere with the US elections to ensure his "friend's" victory?

The CIA was confident of Russia's involvement in hackings which had breached the Democrat Party computers. In a Senate Intelligence Committee meeting in mid-December they confirmed the information. On the other hand, the FBI did not agree. Led by James Comey, that department came under fire by outgoing Senate Majority Leader Harry Reid, who thought that Comey was withholding information about Russia's involvement. After all, Comey obviously did not support the Democratic Party – just look what he did to Clinton just days before Election

PRESIDENCY UNDER PRESSURE

Day. Some people, however, pointed out that the FBI dealt with things in a juristic way to prove criminal intent in court, while the CIA only needed a little evidence in order to advise the government on policy.[10] Trump said the CIA findings were "ridiculous" and that it was just another excuse as to why he won and Hillary lost. He also said there was no way to really know if Russia did the hacks.[11] The story continued to run on and on.[12]

Trump's choice of cabinet members was one that everyone awaited with tense anticipation. He cautiously rolled out his choices as the days advanced. On November 18, he offered Alabama Senator Jeff Sessions the position of Attorney General. Sessions gladly accepted the offer and said he would do the job with "with an unwavering dedication to fairness and impartiality." On the same day, Trump also offered Kansas Rep. Mike Pompeo the job of CIA director, and retired Lt. Gen. Michael Flynn the role of national security adviser. Both accepted, giving Trump a successful start to his cabinet. No one seemed surprised at these choices and many saw the positions as a reward for loyalty.[13]

On November 23, South Carolina Governor Nikki Haley was his choice as American ambassador to the United Nations. Haley gladly accepted, seeing this as a great opportunity to serve her country. This was an ironic choice especially because she had previously opposed Trump's run for the presidency. Nevertheless, Jason Miller, a spokesman close to Trump, said that the two had "natural chemistry", whatever that meant.[14] At any rate, Trump figured that she would be a great deal maker and that she had proven this with her track record. As one of the first female picks for his cabinet, Haley held an important position, and CNN claimed that this was an attempt by Trump to gain support from minorities and women.[15] Yet another female choice for the cabinet was Betsy DeVos who was named Education Secretary. DeVos was also a longtime critic of Trump, but was apparently seen as an excellent choice in education. She had been a supporter of charter schools and alternative choices to the public-school system.[16]

Finally, on November 21, Trump released a video detailing his policy for his first 100 days in office. He said he would withdraw from the Trans-Pacific Partnership trade deal, eliminate restrictions on shale and clean coal, and protect American infrastructure. Altogether, he reviewed campaign promises and gave a brief glimpse into the ideas that would guide the first part of his presidency. Some media outlets were fascinated at the absence of a mention of building a wall between Mexico and the US or the repeal of Obamacare. Other sources predicted that his plan of defunding sanctuary cities for illegal immigrants would end up in court.[17]

Normally, a president-elect could focus solely on politics, but with Trump, politics mingled with business. The general view of Trump's business and potential conflicts as president arose immediately following the election. Trump's children were already involved in the transition team and the rumor was that he would place his children in charge of his corporate empire while serving as president. For many, however, that did not change the conflict at all because Trump would still be interested in the company that made

Presidency Under Pressure

him a billionaire. During the previous 40 years, presidents had placed their business interests in a blind trust, but it did not appear that Trump intended to follow suit. Scandal was sure to come.[18]

For example, some thought Trump's new hotel near the White House in D.C. posed problems. What if someone stayed there, for convenience of course, but was only trying to gain the favor of a President Trump? Others were concerned about Trump's latest meeting with Indian business partners. What if there was a conflict of interest there with regards building projects? Finally, there were concerns that Ivanka Trump was present at a meeting with the president-elect and the Japanese Prime Minister. Only time would tell if Trump would distance himself with his company upon taking office.[19] By the end of November, Trump announced that he would indeed separate with his businesses so that he could focus solely on the nation, saying, "I will be holding a major news conference in New York City with my children on December 15 to discuss the fact that I will be leaving my great business in total in order to fully focus on running the country in order to MAKE AMERICA GREAT AGAIN!"[20] At that point his plan was to pass it over to his children, an idea that he had considered for a while. As the 15th approached, Trump said that he would not have anything to do with management.[21] Then came the news that he was postponing the scheduled announcement, but at the same time he said that his sons Don and Eric, and other executives, would manage his businesses, although "No new deals will be done during my term(s) in office."[22] Right before Christmas, however, he did announce that he would shut down the Trump Foundation in order to avoid conflicts of interest. The media blasted him for trying to do this while it was under investigation. Furthermore, it claimed that Trump didn't even use it for giving his own money, but instead used it to funnel other people's money to pay for things, even a huge painting of himself in one of his sports bars.[23]

Oddly, Trump was also unique in the fact that he had many court cases going while running for president. For example, he had sued chef Jose Andres, for breach of contract since the celebrity chef had a contract to work at Trump's new luxury hotel in Washington D.C. and then backed out. Andres claimed that it was due to disparaging remarks Trump made about Mexicans during the campaign. Just days before the electoral college met, the media announced that Trump would have to sit in on a 7 hour deposition on January 20. Trump tried to get out of it, but the judge declined the request.[24]

The concerns over Trump's conflict of interest continued, however, with people discontent over his worldwide properties and business holdings. Then another problem arose on December 8, with his decision to continue holding the title of executive producer of "The Celebrity Apprentice," which was a spinoff of his extremely popular TV reality show, "The Apprentice." This show was started by Trump and aired for many seasons and it made him widely popular and known worldwide. Most likely, America has "The Apprentice" to thank for making Trump president. At any rate, the show was returning soon with former Governor of California, Arnold Schwarzenegger, as host. Trump would retain his interests in the show.[25] But it only

Presidency Under Pressure

went that far, and Trump stated that he would have "NOTHING" to do with it although he had a "big stake" in it.[26] Critics on the other hand thought this would make Trump, as president, favor NBC over other networks. A former ethics counselor for George Bush said, "We need him to be president — full time — and not to have other contractual commitments elsewhere...He's testing the limits on everything."[27] Not that it caused controversy, but on December 10, Trump also became the first president-elect to attend the annual Army-Navy football game.[28] Indeed he was testing limits, but Trump was the first president in America's history to be quite like he was. Everything was new.

In the second presidential debate, Donald Trump had mentioned the possibility of having the Attorney General look into Clinton's alleged guilt in the whole email scandal if he were elected president. But now, it appeared that now he was reconsidering. He cited other things as more important, telling the Wall Street Journal, "it's not something I've given a lot of thought, because I want to solve health care, jobs, border control, tax reform." This, no doubt, gave a sigh of relief to many Democrats, but there were still those who did not trust Hillary and wanted to see her in prison. Others saw this new position as breaking a campaign promise. "Lock her up" was, after all, a cry chanted at many a Trump rally prior to the election.[29] Instead of locking her up though, he was looking forward to future deals and the White House cabinet positions that needed filled.

CHAPTER III
The Billion Dollar Cabinet

TRUMP'S relationship with the media had already been on shaky ground, but now that he had actually won the election, it seemed that there was a period of relative peace. During the campaign, the New York Times had claimed that Trump's campaign brought in a "tide of racism, anti-Semitism and xenophobia." But now, as president-elect, Trump wanted to meet with the paper and solve differences. Unfortunately, even planning the meeting was blemished with apparent misunderstanding as he first canceled the appointment and then reversed that decision.[30] On the other hand, there were positive elements in the media for Trump. For example, Time made him the "Person of the Year for 2016." In an interview, Trump showed his agreement with the selection, saying "to be on the cover of Time as Person of the Year is a tremendous honor." But he did not agree with the subtitle, which stated that he was the "President of the Divided States of America," saying that it was already divided before and that it would be his job to unite it again. Personally though, Trump was no stranger to being on the cover of Time, as this was the 10th edition featuring him on it.[1]

Saturday Night Live skits also brushed Trump the wrong way and he said that actor Alec Baldwin's parodies of the president-elect were not funny, tweeting, "Just tried watching Saturday Night Live - unwatchable! Totally biased,

Presidency Under Pressure

not funny and the Baldwin impersonation just can't get any worse. Sad." Baldwin responded that he would stop the impersonations if Trump released his tax records. Their exchange prompted one individual, described as an "atheist, civil rights activist, musician and trans-woman," to vent disgust for Trump in an epic Twitter rant which gained over 200,000 likes.[2]

Regardless of criticism, Trump's win had an amazing influence on business in America even before the month of November was over. By November 22, the DOW closed at a record high of 19,023, reaching over 19,000 for the first time. In fact, it rose 667 points since the elections only two weeks before. There was definitely a boost to the economy, or at least a perceived boost, and the Dow continued to climb, reaching a new record again and again.[3] Companies viewed a Trump presidency as one filled with tax cuts and incentives for business.[4] On the other hand, in the first days of December, Trump came out with a proposed 35% tax on companies that move jobs out of the country, saying, "any business that leaves our country for another country, fires its employees, builds a new factory or plant in the other country, and then thinks it will sell its product back into the U.S. without retribution or consequence, is WRONG!"[5] House speaker Paul Ryan indicated that he would not support such a proposal.[6]

Already, even before November was out, Trump negotiated a deal with Carrier air conditioner manufacturing company to keep 1,000 jobs in the US rather than sending them to Mexico. Vice President-elect Mike Pence was in a position to give tax breaks to Carrier, since he was still governor of Indiana. MSNBC, however, added that Pence was making the taxpayers of that state pay to keep Carrier there. Also getting on the action was Nabisco, which looked forward to the Trump administration and "having a constructive dialogue about policies of interest to our business." Likewise, Ford Motor Company told Trump they would be keeping their Lincoln plant in Kentucky.[7] Later on, this had repercussions in Mexico, where it was claimed that Trump took 3,600 Ford jobs back to the US.[8]

Former Democratic presidential candidate Bernie Sanders saw these kinds of deals as a threat to American jobs since other companies would now feel that they could make deals by simply threatening to leave the US.[9] As the deal with Carrier unfolded, however, no one really knew the details.[10] Eventually it was revealed that Carrier got some 6 million dollars in tax incentives with work training grants of 1 million. Trump and Pence made a point of visiting the factory to solidify the move.[11] The former Democratic presidential candidate criticized this as "crony capitalism" and others criticized it as well, one saying Trump was negotiating with businesses "outside of the rule of law and bureaucratic procedure."[12]

It was reported that Trump's goals included "a pledge to create 25 million jobs and push growth to 4 percent annually."[13] If he was able to do this, then he would do more than Obama succeeded in doing. Nevertheless, supporters of Obama maintained that while Trump may have kept 1,000 jobs in the US, the outgoing president had created hundreds of thousands of new jobs and the president-elect had a long way to go. Several days after the Carrier deal, Trump's victory was criticized for getting the numbers wrong. Trump had eventually claimed 1,150 jobs saved, but apparently it was only 800. The media had a brief heyday with this one.[14] In late December Trump was at it again, and claimed to be bringing 5,000 offshore jobs with Sprint back into the country, in addition to 3,000 new jobs for OneWeb. The media also questioned these numbers and the significance of the deal, but the fact was, there were things happening in the job/business sector due to Trump's presidency. Sprint's stock rose due to the announcement.[15]

Over the days of November, Trump's choices kept piling up and everyone waited in expectation over his choice of Secretary of State. By December 1, people believed his top picks were Rudy Giuliani, Mitt Romney, or David Petraeus. Romney seemed most prominent as perceived by the media, although die-hard conservatives saw him as a choice which contradicted the values of conservative Americans. At one Trump rally in Ohio, a group shouted, "No Romney! No Romney!"[16] In the meantime, Jeff Sessions was slammed as a racist due to previous "racially insensitive" remarks he had made years before. Nevertheless, he defended himself at the time, saying, "I am not the Jeff Sessions my detractors have tried to create...I am not a racist. I am not insensitive to blacks."[17] Georgia Representative Tom Price, chosen as Secretary of Health and Human Services was also seen as a fringe selection as he had been firmly opposed to abortion, gay marriage, and Obamacare. As Secretary of Transportation, Trump selected Elaine Chao, married to Senate Majority Leader Mitch McConnell, who had served eight years under President Bush as labor secretary.[18]

THE BILLION DOLLAR CABINET

Trump then chose Steven Mnuchin as Treasury Secretary and Wilbur Ross Jr. as head of the Commerce Department. The latter was a billionaire investor and was slated to get better trade deals for the US.[19] The former had been a Goldman Sachs investor and hedge fund manager. Trump also chose Todd Ricketts, owner of the Chicago Cubs, as the deputy commerce secretary. The group Trump was surrounding himself with was turning out to be the wealthiest Cabinet in America's history. The New York Times saw this as a signal of Trump's embracing Wall Street, yet Mnuchin declared that there would be no tax breaks for the wealthy, but for the working class.[20] Another Goldman Sachs connection came in mid-December with the choice of Gary Cohn as the director of the National Economic Council and the president's assistant for economic policy. Some were shocked at this choice because Cohn was the president of Goldman Sachs and because Trump had previously criticized his former opponent Sen. Ted Cruz's connection with the company.[21]

Trump's pick for secretary of defense was a surprise for some but not for others. He was retired Marine Gen. James Mattis, nicknamed "Mad Dog" for his tough talk and being such a hardliner. Trump indicated this pick at a rally prior to officially making it. This choice, however, required a waiver from Congress, since Mattis retired in 2013 and the law required one to be retired from active duty for seven years before taking up the office. Mattis became famous during the second battle at Fallujah and continued to lead the military in Iraq and Afghanistan. He is known for such tough-guy comments as, "Be polite, be professional, but have a plan to kill everybody you meet."[22] On December 7, Trump

PRESIDENCY UNDER PRESSURE

officially announced Mattis as his pick. The general graciously accepted, as long as the waiver passed and Congress confirmed his position. Trump responded, "You're going to get that waiver...If you don't get that waiver, there are going to be a lot of angry people." The House GOP immediately inserted language into a necessary spending bill that would expedite the waiver.[23]

Yet another general, John Kelly, was chosen for Secretary of Homeland Security. Kelly, who was 66 and retired at the time, had run the United States Southern Command, meaning that he was already experienced with problems south of the American border, thus immigration. He had dealt with drug trafficking and was aware of possible connections between terrorists and smuggling. The media reported that he was "blunt-spoken and popular with military personnel." Some, however, were surprised that Trump had not chosen a person more radical in anti-immigration.[24] He was supposed to be against immigration. After all, in what was one of his less "presidential" moments, hadn't Trump been humored at a reporter's idea that the Statue of Liberty (which welcomed immigrants) be replaced with a statue of his wife Melania sticking up her middle finger at Europe? "Great idea!...I got to tell you, Americans will love it. Europe won't. Who cares what Europe thinks? Screw Europe." The irony, of course, being that Melania hailed from Slovenia.[25]

A few days after announcing Mattis, Trump chose former presidential candidate and adversary, Ben Carson, to lead the Department of Housing and Urban Development. This was an interesting choice, fueled by Carson's concern for inner city communities. Trump said that Carson was a good pick because the neurosurgeon and author had a "brilliant mind and is passionate about strengthening communities and families within those communities." This choice was criticized. One opponent said it was "surprising and concerning," since Carson lacked experience in such matters.[26]

Trump's next pick was Scott Pruitt, attorney general for Oklahoma, to head the Environmental Protection Agency. Now this surprised the media because Pruitt was not known as a supporter of the EPA, and what was even worse, he was strongly biased against it. In fact, he had sued the EPA before. The Washington Post said it was "a move signaling an assault on President Obama's climate change and environmental legacy." The Trump team, however, saw this selection as a reasonable one and one that would end the terrible waste of money that the EPA had been responsible for. It would also bolster business.[27] The subsequent expected pick for the Interior Department was Washington Republican Rep. Cathy McMorris Rodgers. The media reported that she supported hydropower and would "open up federal lands and waters to fossil-fuel development and reverse environmental policies the Obama administration has pursued over the past eight years." On the other hand, she as a choice was not too radical, seeing how she was already a high-ranking Republican and part of the "establishment."[28] Perhaps she would be a balance to Pruitt's apparent radicalism.

People could easily see that all of Trump's choices were totally new. The Wall Street Journal wrote an article

PRESIDENCY UNDER PRESSURE

outlining the apparent fact that Trump was assembling a cabinet which would deregulate America over the following years.[29]

Then, on December 9, it came out that Trump was going to select Rex Tillerson, chairman and CEO of ExxonMoblie, as Secretary of State. This seemed a shock to the casual news reader, as the name never came up before. The leaked information soon became tenable with Trump tweeting two days later, "Whether I choose him or not for 'State'- Rex Tillerson, the Chairman & CEO of ExxonMobil, is a world class player and deal-maker. Stay tuned!" On the same day, Trump praised Tillerson on Fox News saying, "He does massive deals in Russia. He does massive deals – for the company, not for himself, for the company." Former presidential candidate Marco Rubio didn't like the connection with Russia, saying that he did not think being a "friend of Vladimir" was a desirable quality for the Secretary of State. Sen. John McCain didn't like it either. Apparently Tillerson had made oil deals which had directly benefitted the Russian government, and also received from the Russian government the highest non-citizen award possible. The announcement also trailed news that Rudy Giuliani was out of the game for Secretary of State.[30] On December 13, Trump confirmed Tillerson's pick with a tweet, "I have chosen one of the truly great business leaders of the world, Rex Tillerson, Chairman and CEO of ExxonMobil, to be Secretary of State." Former Secretary of Defense Robert Gates as well as Former Secretary of State Condoleezza Rice endorsed Trump's pick as did former US secretary of state Henry Kissinger.[31]

The Billion Dollar Cabinet

Some were happy with the choices Trump made, while others were not. By December 10, his team comprised "three military generals, two governors, one state attorney general, two congressmen, one senator, and three current or former Goldman Sachs bankers, among a host of business executives and billionaires." It was a strange mixture and one which seemed to not stack up to Trump's campaign promise to "drain the swamp." Many Republicans, however, saw this as a swamp drain. It was certainly the first time so many businessmen were brought into the president's cabinet.[32] By December 16, there were 20 Cabinet pics, yet none were Democrats. This was said to be the first time since Franklin D. Roosevelt that a president had not chosen a member of the opposing party to be in his Cabinet.[33] One of the president-elect's main slogans had been "drain the swamp," meaning he was going to get rid of shady lobbying in Washington D.C. Newt Gingrich made the mistake of claiming that Trump had decided not to use the slogan anymore, and then next day Trump blasted back that he would indeed use it.[34]

The Cabinet picks moved on in mid-month. Former Texas Gov. Rick Perry was chosen head of the Department of Energy. At least he was a real politician. At first he did not support Trump's bid for presidency, but eventually got on board. Trump said Perry would "take advantage of our huge natural resource deposits to make America energy independent and create vast new wealth for our nation." This choice apparently would blend well with the Pruitt and McMorris Rodgers picks made for other departments.[35] As the new year arrived, Trump's choice for secretary of agriculture narrowed down to Sonny Perdue III, the former governor of Georgia.[36]

The choices for cabinet positions seemed to overwhelmingly come from the business rather than the political field. On December 21 Trump chose Carl Icahn, a fellow billionaire, to be a White House advisor. This hedge fund investor was an interesting choice due to Icahn's connection with the oil industry. Some feared that he might use his influence to benefit his business deals. For the same advisory position Trump also picked Peter Navarro, a business professor at the University of California, who would also head the National Trade Council. The media explained that Navarro had already been involved with Trump and had proposed such things as "ripping up long-standing agreements with Mexico, slapping double-digit tariffs on imports from China and punishing companies that outsource manufacturing jobs."[37] One choice which did not come as a surprise and added variety was Kellyanne Conway as White House counselor. She had done a great job as campaign manager and now would continue to help as Trump went on to Washington D.C.[38] These new choices only confirmed the direction of the Trump transition towards less globalization and a stronger America.

CHAPTER IV
The Recount

OF COURSE, Obama and Trump did not see eye to eye even though they had to meet and discuss the transition of power. In fact, Trump challenged much of Obama's work done as president. One example of their differences was the stance on Cuba. Obama opened up relations between the US and Cuba, but Trump promised to close that door. Fidel Castro, the Communist dictator of Cuba died on November 26, and Trump simply tweeted "Fidel Castro is dead!" On the other hand, Obama was friendlier and said that history will be the judge of Castro.[1]

Trump's rise in America was seen as a populist movement and it gave an example to other countries of the world that the Right could win even against the odds. In Europe it bolstered hope in countries such as Italy where Beppe Grillo, a comedian turned politician, was a rising populist leader.[2] Trump seemed different from Obama in all things. Even his choice for ambassador to Israel was different in that David M. Friedman, according to Time Magazine, fit with the policies of Israeli Prime Minister Benjamin Netanyahu like a key fits a lock. That is, he supported settlement and a no Palestinian State policy.[3] In fact, in later December, Trump pushed for Obama to veto a UN resolution to end Israeli settlements. Perhaps this had

Presidency Under Pressure

some effect since the US abstained from voting. Despite this intervention, the resolution passed.[4]

On December 2, Trump even had an unprecedented phone call from the president of Taiwan, Tsai Ing-wen, who congratulated him, but this was the first time heads of state from the two countries had spoken since 1979 when the US broke diplomatic ties with Taiwan in favor of China. China was furious over the exchange, and Foreign Minister Wang Yi responded that this was a "little trick pulled off by Taiwan," saying "we don't want to see this political foundation disturbed and damaged."[5] Trump had blasted China throughout his campaign and it was not much of a surprise that he would speak with Taiwan. A few days later, Trump's senior advisor KellyAnne Conway said, "It's just a phone call…President-elect Trump is not out there making policy or policy prescriptions." Nevertheless, the call made quite a diplomatic splash.[6] Trump continued to speak of China in December, accusing it of things such as "massive theft of intellectual property…unfair taxes on our companies…not helping with the menace of North Korea like they should." He proposed a relationship where China would not exploit US companies at the expense of US jobs.[7]

Trump also decried the exorbitant cost of the new Air Force One order placed by Obama with Boeing. The current contract when he was elected was set at $170 million, but the Air Force had planned on a total of $2.1 billion by 2021. On December 6, however, the news reported Trump's tweet, "Boeing is building a brand new 747 Air Force One for future presidents, but costs are out of control, more than $4 billion. Cancel order!" That just seemed outrageous to the

THE RECOUNT

president-elect, and it would be paid by American tax dollars.[8] A few days later he also criticized the Lockheed Martin F-35 fighter jet program, saying that the costs were "out of control" and that he would begin saving money for the US government. Perhaps more interesting was the result of his tweet, which caused Lockheed Martin's stock to fall 4%.[9] Within weeks these tweets were followed with other news. Boeing chief executive Dennis Muilenburg met with Trump and then stated afterwards that his company would lower the price tag. Trump also began looking for alternatives to the F-35, possibly a version of the F-18 Super Hornet.[10] His comments made Lockheed Martin's stock to fall yet again.[11]

On December 5, it was announced that Trump and his daughter Ivanka met with former Vice President Al Gore to discuss climate change. The media seemed hopeful that these talks might change Trump's mind, who actually denied climate change and thought it was a hoax. The media claimed "it may come down to who has his ear last." Perhaps, but Trump had long been at variance with climate change supporters.[12] A few days later he said on the topic, "I'm still open-minded. Nobody really knows" (if climate change is real).[13] Even in December supporters of the issue were attacking Trump's team for sending out a questionnaire to Department of Energy employees.[14] Nonetheless, while the president-elect may have considered this a hoax, he did not support fake news, and the following day, Michael Flynn Jr., the son of one of his advisors who was helping his father with the transition efforts, was fired for spreading fake news on the web which had led to a pizzeria shooting in Washington D.C.[15] Hillary Clinton came out days later

Presidency Under Pressure

announcing that fake news was becoming an "epidemic" and "it's now clear that so-called fake news can have real-world consequences."[16]

Yet another turn of events occurred as the month of November came to a close, this was efforts to call a recount of votes in three important states where Trump narrowly won. The odd thing is that it was not Clinton who called for the recount. That would have perhaps been seen as poor taste, especially since her team had already accepted the election results as the choice of the American people. Plus, with Trump having declined to accept the election results in the third debate, she could not now do the same thing openly. However, it was the Green Party candidate Jill Stein who called for the recount. Shortly after Stein's declaration to call a recount the Clinton team said it would participate in the recount. After all, in Michigan Trump won by less than 12,000 votes, in Wisconsin by less than 30,000 , and in Pennsylvania by less than 70,000 votes. If Clinton won these three states she would have enough electoral votes to win the presidency.[17] Overall, Trump responded to these efforts by saying that it was a scam, saying it was only a way for Stein "to fill her coffers with money."[18] Furthermore he used this as an opportunity to claim that there were millions who voted illegally for Clinton and that if these numbers were deducted from Clinton's totals then Trump would have won the popular vote. It was intriguing, however, that the Clinton camp seemed to assume that the number of votes would somehow increase for her alone, while omitting the possibility that Trump might actually get more votes out of a recount.[19]

The Recount

As the recount efforts rolled on and Stein collected enough money to pay for the recount in the three states, tension between the Trump and Clinton camps increased. The general view was that Clinton was directing the recount behind the scenes. After all, Stein could in no way benefit from the recount, receiving only about 1 percent of the vote in Michigan, Pennsylvania and Wisconsin. Clinton would be the only candidate to benefit and could possible retake all three states. Clinton's group, however, denied having a role in the initial recount efforts, but this did not deter Trump and his lawyers, who began legal proceedings in an effort to stop the recount.

The New York Times reported on December 2 that Trump's team claimed the recount would stall the Electoral College which would be meeting in two weeks to conclude the election process, thus the recount should not proceed because it would take too long to finish. But regardless of the intervention, counting started in Pennsylvania and Wisconsin. On the other hand, it seemed that Stein had waited too long to declare a recount for Michigan and the count there stalled.[20] Then she turned to the Federal Court and a judge ordered the recount to begin by noon on Monday, December 5. That day, Stein held a press conference in front of Trump Tower in New York to support her move, where Trump supporters also came to picket. In the end, Trump won the Michigan by only 10,704 votes, however, no one expected the recounts to change the outcome of the overall election results.[21] All these efforts in Michigan came to an end two days later, when the same judge sided with a state appeals court decision that ended the recount because Stein was not an "aggrieved candidate."[22]

Stein made an appeal but the court declined.[23] In Pennsylvania the recount also stalled for the most part, since there was little evidence of voter fraud.

The news came on December 12 that the recount in Wisconsin was done. Trump won again. Pennsylvania also verified the vote results with a Trump win. So the recount did not amount to much, except to call into question the voting process and to provide some media distractions leading up to the electoral college meeting.[24] On the other hand, it kept an eye on Trump's Electoral College win, since he did not win the popular vote and now disgruntled people were clamoring to abolish it. NPR news aired reports on it. The main gist went like this: the Electoral College is an "anachronistic element of our democracy that gave him the win."[25] The New York Times speculated on whether or not Trump was a threat to democracy.[26]

Then celebrities took a stand against Trump, while careful to not tell electors to support Hillary. Instead, they told electors to vote their conscience and appoint someone who was qualified to be president. As Martin Sheen put it, "As you know, our founding fathers built the electoral college to safeguard the American people from the dangers of a demagogue and to ensure that the presidency only goes to someone who is, to an eminent degree, endowed with the requisite qualifications."[27] A demagogue, or as the original Greek suggests, a leader of the people, is someone who goes directly to the people and that was a hallmark of Trump's campaign. While Trump would not have agreed with celebrities, he certainly believed in going to the people. In the days leading up to the Electoral College vote he

THE RECOUNT

continued rallies, and as the Washington Post reported, it allowed him to bypass the press and communicate directly with his supporters. One of the latter thought it was the right way to go, saying of the press, "I know they lie...You want to hear the truth? Come out here and listen to him."[28]

With this hurdle of a recount finally over, Hillary supporters now moved onto a new possible method of defeating Trump: criticize the way he won in an effort to sway members of the Electoral College to not vote for him. The argument went that Russia was responsible for the hacks which discredited Hillary Clinton, causing her to lose. Therefore, her loss was invalid. There were those who questioned this logic by asking why it mattered, since, if the things which discredited her were true then who cares where the information comes from. The real unspoken purpose, however, must have been to connect Trump himself with Russia and the internet attacks, since it was he who benefitted from the hackings.

CHAPTER V
From Russia With Love

ELECTORS were greatly pressured to distance themselves from Donald Trump during the days leading up to their official vote for the president. People who opposed Trump or supported Clinton tried to get them to at least not vote for Trump, and although this tactic seemed impossible to succeed, there was a lot of coverage in the media for such a move. There were celebrities voicing their opinions and interviews with people trying to convince electors to switch. One was swayed. Christopher Suprun, a Republican elector in Texas, said he would not vote for Trump.[1] There were claims that some electors received death threats if they voted Trump.[2] Electors were not prepared for the extra work and stress of electing Donald Trump as president. One elector's email rose from 300 messages a day around election time to 3000 right before the voting. They were constantly being bombarded with tips, suggestions, threats, complaints, and pleas to not vote for Trump. But for most, they would vote for Trump since their state had gone that direction.[3]

While all of this was going on, the issue of Russia being responsible for the email hacks prior to the elections would not go away. NBC News reported on December 15 that intelligence officials told them that they were highly confident that Putin was "personally involved" in the hacks. The next day President-elect Trump sent a tweet which the Huffington Post said, "suggested that whoever stole tens of

Presidency Under Pressure

thousands of emails from top Democratic officials and leaked them online was actually doing America a favor." Trump, however, was only pointing out that the emails proved that the Democrats were involved in some shady behavior during the elections. Either way, the Democrats viewed Russia's involvement as an attack on America's democracy.[4]

President Obama responded to the Russian problem with force, saying that America would take action for it. He saw a threat to democracy too. Obviously, the hack was directed at Hillary, and he acknowledged that "in fact what the Russian hack had done was create more problems for the Clinton campaign than it had for the Trump campaign." He also withheld the fact that the email scandals focused weeks and months during the election campaign on issues that had a negative impact on the Democratic Party and Hillary Clinton. It appeared, however, that Trump's tweet was indirectly trying to state that regardless of where the information came from, if they pointed out "illegal" acts, then in a way who cares where it came from. Obama obviously disagreed with him.[5] He was terrified at the prospect that America could be losing American values and gliding towards those of Russia.[6] Like the president, Hillary's campaign chief John Podesta spoke up right before the Electoral College vote saying that Russia "intervened" in the US elections, in response to the question of whether or not 2016 was a "free and fair" election. The involvement of Russia was a big deal now. He wanted electors to be informed prior to voting. But Conway, said that the whole thing was ridiculous. She retorted that a coordinated connection between the Trump campaign and Russia was

From Russia with Love

"inaccurate and false ... dangerous. And it does undermine our democracy." So, while the Democrats saw Russia hacks as a threat to democracy, she saw an attack on a legitimate Trump presidency as a threat to democracy.[7] Nevertheless, Trump's Chief of Staff, Priebus, said that Trump would accept the supposed involvement of Russia if all of the intelligence agencies "would get together, put out a report, show the American people that they are actually on the same page." This was reported one day prior to the Electoral College vote.[8] Trump himself simply stated that if his supporters "acted and threatened people like those who lost the election are doing, they would be scorned & called terrible names!"[9]

On December 19, the Electoral College cast their votes, and Donald Trump was elected the 45th president of the United States of America. Only two Republican electors chose to not vote Trump, and four Democrat electors changed their votes, but for the most part electors followed tradition. Trump received 304 and Clinton 227. This sealed Trump's win of the presidency.[10] One of the dissenting Republicans said Trump would be impeached within his first year as president.[11] Those who supported Clinton were devastated. One article sadly noted, with "Trump entering the Oval Office, hope is dead. Or worse, right now hope looks foolish." People compared the situation with the "bleak" newly-released Star Wars film, Rogue One.[12]

Nonetheless, there were those who still vowed to fight Trump. In his own way, Obama fought on, with 78 pardons and 153 commutations on the same day in December, setting a single day record for commutations. The media claimed that Trump's election brought a new "urgency" to pardons and commutations. In fact, the trend continued, and three days before leaving office he drove the total number of commutations to 1,385, setting a record over President Woodrow Wilson's 1,366. Among those who benefitted was Chelsea Manning, the Army intelligence analyst convicted of disclosing information to WikiLeaks. There was even talk of Edward Snowden being pardoned.[13]

Obama also placed an indefinite ban on oil drilling in huge areas of the Arctic and Atlantic oceans.[14] The Washington Post claimed that this meant four years of thwarting the battle against global warming.[15] Liberals hoped that Obama would continue to lead them against whatever might be coming against them in a Trump presidency.[16] At any rate, they still had a month to go before inauguration and they were not done fighting yet. For Republicans, however, it seemed they now accepted Trump.

It was rather interesting that Trump continued to use private sector security personnel in addition to the Secret Service people who were assigned to him in November. It was called unprecedented that a president-elect continue using private security after winning the elections. It was even said that Trump would continue to do so, at least in part, after being sworn in as president. There were complaints that it was risky, confusing, and even "playing with fire." In part, it might be understandable, with all of the protests against his bid and win that he would want more security around. He also wanted loyal people whom he had employed for years already as security. In a way, it seemed only a matter of time before people started protesting this as a "personal army."[17]

FROM RUSSIA WITH LOVE

Trump definitely seemed a tough guy. When Russian President Putin said that his country would increase is nuclear weapon potential, Trump responded in kind, saying that the US must "greatly strengthen and expand" in that field as well "until such time as the world comes to its senses regarding nukes."[18]

Immediately after the Electoral College vote there was a lull in the media concerning Trump and any controversy. This was a nice break. On the other hand it all began again after a few days. Within a week, Trump was making comments about foreign policy which irritated Obama and others. He signaled an increase in nuclear weapons. He told Obama to veto the UN resolution on curbing Israeli settlement. But Ben Rhodes, Obama's deputy national-security adviser retorted, "There's one president at a time…it's important that the world understands who is speaking on behalf of the United States until Jan. 20." Obviously these words came from Obama to be relayed to Trump – not so fast buddy.[19] Trump, however, was disappointed with the UN, saying that it was turning out to be a club where people got together to "talk and have a good time." He just urged Israel to hang in there until January 20.[20]

As if to prove his current position as president, Obama seemed to be picking fights with Trump. Republicans felt that he was hurrying with "midnight regulations," that is, last minute executive orders and such, since he had many left over projects which Hillary Clinton would now not be finishing for him. Former House Speaker Newt Gingrich said Obama was in a "desperate frenzy."[21] The battle

Presidency Under Pressure

continued on December 26, when Obama claimed that had he run for a third term he would have won. Trump responded, saying that there was no way Obama would have won.[22] Then a couple days later at the Pearl Harbor memorial, Obama seemed to take jabs at Trump's ideas. The president-elect responded, "Doing my best to disregard the many inflammatory President O statements and roadblocks. Thought it was going to be a smooth transition - NOT!"[23] So it seemed that things were taking a turn for the worse by the end of 2016. More shocking was Obama's December 28 creation of two new national monuments protecting 1.35 million acres around the Bears Ears Buttes in Utah and approximately 300,000 acres at Gold Butte in Nevada. The New York Times called this an attempt to nail down his legacy as the environmental president.[24] He also kept transferring detainees from Guantanamo Bay, although Trump wanted them to remain there.[25]

Democrats in general were looking for ways to block Trump's cabinet appointments too, but the media commented that they had changed filibuster rules in 2013, which effectively blocked them from doing so, now that Republicans controlled the senate.[26] At the very least, they were looking for ways to preserve Obama's legacy. Obamacare was on the line too, as Republicans prepared to repeal it and replace it. Yet they did not agree on how to do it.[27] This came as Trump was making his final Cabinet choices. The New York Times reported that the president-elect chose Wall Street lawyer Walter Clayton to lead the Securities and Exchange Commission, saying that he was "the insider's insider — a deal maker." This was supposed to signal an easing on regulations.[28]

FROM RUSSIA WITH LOVE

While all of this was occurring, the whole issue of Russia being involved in the US election process came back to the forefront. The media announced that Obama was armed with more concrete information and he therefore announced on December 29 the placement of sanctions on Russian intelligence officials and the expulsion of 35 Russian diplomats suspected of spying. Trump was reserved and waited to respond.[29] Some thought that Obama's actions were politically motivated. Surprisingly, Putin did not respond by expelling American diplomats, but intended to wait for Trump to take office. The latter said that this was very smart.[30] As things unfolded, it seemed that Trump did not really believe that Russia made the hacks. The media portrayed Trump as disputing intelligence on Russian hacking, but he stated "I want them to be sure, because it's a pretty serious charge," citing the weapons of mass destruction charge which led to the invasion of Iraq in 2003.[31] Interestingly, in a piece announcing an upcoming press conference on January 11, Trump's first after winning the election, Fox News reminded readers how Trump had said in the previous conference on July 27, "I will tell you this, Russia: If you're listening, I hope you're able to find the 30,000 emails that are missing." Of course, that was supposed to be a joke, but many took him seriously.[32]

Intelligence apparently proved that the WikiLeaks source for the emails was Russia. It also, however, proved that none of the emails were forged, which was a significant admission, since Democrats had denied the validity of them. WikiLeaks founder, Julian Assange, asserted on January 4 that his source for the emails was not Russia, or any state party. Despite this, and Trump's concurring opinion at the time, the United States government continued to assert Russia's role in the hacking.[33] In fact, many criticized Trump. The director of national intelligence, James Clapper Jr., indicated that disparagement of the intelligence community was wrong. Senator John McCain discredited Assange's claim that Russia was not involved.[34] On the other hand, it was said that the Russians cheered when they heard that Trump won.[35] Furthermore, the declassified version of the intelligence document claimed that Russian President Putin himself ordered a cyber campaign, at first directed to hurt a Clinton presidency, but then to actively support Trump as presidential candidate.[36] The day following its release, Trump simply said that the Russian activity had no direct effect on the election. He also said that the US should work on a good relationship with Russia – those who thought otherwise were "fools."[37]

Connected with the intelligence information mentioned above was the revelation that the Russians had also collected some rather salacious information concerning the president-elect. This information was supposedly collected into a document of questionable veracity by a former British M16 agent and the US government was aware of its contents. Armed with that information, the Russian government could allegedly blackmail Trump, as the stories in it were not of the kind a person would want floating around the web.[38] And yet, someone leaked the "Russia dossier" to the media. CNN was the first to report on it and indicate the contents, but it was Buzzfeed that published the entire package of 35 pages. Within minutes the news was all over social media. The Kremlin said that this was totally false - a "complete fabrication and utter nonsense." Trump said the same thing

FROM RUSSIA WITH LOVE

about it and expressed his shock in several tweets that someone in the American intelligence community could even leak the supposed actions of Trump while visiting Russia in 2013.[39] The negative reaction was immediate because the dossier appeared too fantastic to be true and was unverified news. CNN quickly backpedaled, but the damage was already done. The fake news controversy was thus born.[40]

CHAPTER VI
You Are Fake News

POLITICS shifted several situations as the days led up to inauguration day. The wall on the Mexican-American border was at issue. Trump decided that the US could build the wall first, "for the sake of speed," then make Mexico pay for it afterwards. At a cost of up to 10 billion dollars, it was no small task.[1] Also an upcoming issue was the confirmation hearings for Trump's Cabinet choices. Would there be trouble? After all, Trump told Obama's ambassadors to leave their positions by inauguration day, which the media tried to portray as an attack on Obama although the latter did the same thing to President Bush.[2] On the other side, Vice President Joe Biden tried to convince Democratic senators from preventing Trump's supreme court nominee from having a hearing. Nevertheless, Democrat Senate Minority Leader Charles Schumer said his party "would oppose a Supreme Court nominee they didn't agree with 'tooth and nail'."[3] That seemed to be the most common attitude. Closer to home, opponents indicated that if Trump followed through with his idea of making Jared Kushner, his son-in-law, a senior advisor then he would really run into trouble – that was nepotism. As for Cabinet choices though, Sen. Jeff Sessions ran into trouble from the start of his nomination hearing before senate. Several members of Congress opposed him

PRESIDENCY UNDER PRESSURE

saying that he was a racist. The NAACP agreed with that accusation.[4]

Trump now planned his first press conference since July 27 the previous year. This was the event that the nation was waiting for. He had delayed the conference scheduled for December 15, and finally, on January 11, it took place. He explained how he would separate himself from his company to serve as America's president. Firstly, he passed control of his company over to his sons Donald Jr. and Eric Trump. He also resigned all positions and placed it in a trust. His motivation was to remove any question of conflicts of interest. He spoke of many other things, including the issue of jobs being brought back the US and the poor deals made by America with foreign countries. His business decisions seemed reasonable to supporters, but the Washington Post criticized his conference as did the New York Times. The former fact checked his speech, and the latter said that the media better figure out how to deal with Trump quickly since he used the opportunity to berate the press – again. NBC News published interviews with people from several foreign nations, and for the most part they were concerned about negative consequences of a Trump presidency.[5]

The most memorable incident of the press conference was the president-elect's interaction with CNN reporter Jim Acosta, who attempted to ask Trump a question. The president-elect, however, would not take a question from that news organization's reporter, since CNN had been involved in publishing the Russia dossier that Trump had already called utter nonsense. There followed a lively exchange between the two, with Trump pointing towards him saying,

"YOU ARE FAKE NEWS"

"you are fake news." CNN reacted indignantly to the incident and it was not long before other media outlets joined together to oppose Trump's accusation of fake news.[6]

Hearings for Cabinet posts continued during the week leading up to inauguration day. Rex Tillerson was grilled by senators during his hearing. Former Republican presidential candidate Marco Rubio questioned him about Russia's threat to the US, of course, the real question was to what extent did Tillerson's relationship with Russia influence him. USA Today reported that Tillerson thought Russia was a danger because it wanted respect. When asked about sanctions as a political tool, he responded that sanctions on Russia "have a role" but on the other hand, having "ineffective sanctions is worse than having no sanctions at all. It runs the risk of sending a weak signal." Other political ideas on the table included China and ISIS. Tillerson said that China's activity in the South China Sea was illegal and that ISIS posed the greatest threat the US national security.[7] Gen. James Mattis sent the same message at his hearing for defense secretary: "I think [the world order is] under the biggest attack since World War II ... from Russia, from terrorist groups and with what China is doing in the South China Sea." Mattis was questioned by Senator John McCain about Russia and other threats. Yet for the most part, Mattis seemed to have support and easily received his waiver to take office by 81 to 17 votes.[8] If Mattis received a relatively successful hearing, Betsy DeVos's hearing for Education Secretary was hardly an instantaneous success. Her's was a grilling session and Democrats said she was unfit for the job. Republicans supported her as a bold reformer, but the hearing was contentious.[9]

Presidency Under Pressure

As demonstrated in the CNN "fake news" incident, the Trump administration's relationship with reporters was sketchy. In fact, there was talk of moving reporters from the White House, or at least moving their location. Reporters became nervous and defensive, vowing to fight against this infringement on freedom of the press. Reince Priebus, chief of staff nominee, said that they were only thinking of changing the room where press conferences took place since it was too small, yet it appeared that there could be more drastic changes. Time would tell.[10] Yet, perhaps the relationship with Trump and Fox News would grow closer, since the "Fox News Effect" had led to greater support for Trump, and the majority of Trump supporters (40%) got their news there.[11] CNN was obviously out. NBC was in trouble too, since it questioned Trump's effect on bringing jobs back to the US, saying his impact in that area was "very small or non-existent." NBC's "Today" show got the fake news accusation for that one.[12]

Trump critics, however, were not only counted among the media. Celebrities were vocal about their opinions. At the Golden Globes Meryl Streep nearly cried talking about her disappointment with Trump. Host Jimmy Fallon poked fun at him. The Huffington Post reported that Frank Sinatra's daughter "destroyed" Trump with a negative tweet when she heard that the Trumps would dance to one of her father's songs on inauguration day. Actor Alec Baldwin mocked Trump in the first Saturday Night Live skit of 2017, playing the president-elect at his January news conference.[13] But not all aimed their criticism on Trump. He did have supporters, or at least those who wanted to move on. Actress Nicole Kidman was one of these few voices in her field saying,

"You Are Fake News"

"[Trump is] now elected and we, as a country, need to support whoever is the president."[14] Rapper Kanye West voiced his support for Trump.[15] Yet it seemed that anyone from the upper echelons of society who supported Trump was in hot water. Linda Bean, granddaughter and co-owner of L.L. Bean, supported Trump but was attacked for doing so. Grabyourwallet.org called for a boycott of her company as well as others that sold Trump products or supported him.[16]

Speaking of a boycott, the civil rights icon and congressman John Lewis said he would not attend the inauguration ceremonies because he did not view Trump as a legitimate president due to Russia's meddling with US elections. Of course, Trump twittered back, criticizing Lewis for his boycott and other things. People came out to support Lewis, including Nancy Pelosi. Soon, it was reported that more than 50 Democrats would not attend the inauguration. It seemed that this was the first time this ever happened. Nonetheless, Lewis did not attend the 2001 Bush inauguration, and 80 had not attended Nixon's in 1973.[17] Yet, Republicans were dismayed at all of the talk of boycotts and the lack of support for the electoral process. When Obama and Clinton were elected, they didn't take to the streets and protest, nor come up with boycotts, according to those interviewed by USA Today. But it was acknowledged that it would take much time to heal the scars of a divided United States. Trump hoped to signal a healing with his choices of prayer leaders at the inauguration which included an African-American church leader, a Jewish rabbi, a Catholic archbishop, and the son of Billy Graham.[18]

Presidency Under Pressure

In the few remaining days leading up to inauguration day there were a few interesting political developments. Trump spoke of a replacement healthcare plan for Obamacare that would provide insurance for everyone. This appealed to many, but how would Republicans react? On relations with other countries, apparently, the Trump team would attend talks organized by Russia to pursue a ceasefire in Syria – something previously promoted by Obama. Over in Europe, Trump had called NATO "obsolete" since it was not dealing with terror as it should. Instead, the US was pouring more money into it along with a few other countries, than the majority of member countries were. He criticized Germany for allowing so many immigrants into its country. He even hinted at the possibility of extending immigration restrictions to European countries.[19]

The Nation was on edge before the inauguration. Trump definitely had supporters, but there were also those who opposed him. He won the election, but was attacked again and again for doing so. He was called illegitimate. There were protests. Nonetheless, he would be inaugurated as the 45th president of the United States of America on January 20, 2017 and there was nothing that could be done about it. His opposition had tried everything they could. The focus from the election to the electoral college vote was the search to prevent him from actually becoming president. From the electoral college vote to inauguration day was the search to discredit his win. These efforts would probably fail, just as the previous efforts to delegitimize him had failed. The man did have a way with the Press though, who could doubt that? He played them like a musical instrument. If they went out

"YOU ARE FAKE NEWS"

of tune, he re-tuned them. The media reported the news and it was a bumpy trail for the president-elect.

Trump made his own news. It was not necessarily the fault of the media that they had so much fodder on him. He dealt the cards that way. Nonetheless, certain people within those organizations clearly did not like him and spun stories to hurt him as much as possible. Was there positive news about Trump? It seemed that there was very little. Most of it was negative, although it was partly negative due to the conflicts between Trump and his conservative supporters and the Democrats and their liberal supporters. So very few really believed he would ever win the Republican Party nomination as president, and even fewer believed he could beat Hillary Clinton. Yet, here we were – America had a new president and it was Donald Trump. This was an unexpected turn for half of the nation and the path was unknown.

Part II – The First 100 Days

CHAPTER VII
Make America Great Again

PRESIDENT Trump began his inaugural address thus: "We, the citizens of America, are now joined in a great national effort to rebuild our country and to restore its promise for all of our people." It was a momentous occasion for the billionaire turned politician. The first lady, Melania Trump stood next to him as he took the oath of office. Former president and first lady, Barack and Michelle Obama looked on as the torch passed from one administration to the next. It was a rainy overcast day. Thousands watched from the National Mall while millions watched from the comfort of their homes. A large portion of the United States was covered in snow, but for the citizens of the majority of states, the new administration would bring a new-found warmth – hope for the future. This was the sentiment of Trump's closing words: "Together, we will make America strong again. We will make [it] wealthy again. We will make America proud again. We will make America safe again. And yes, together, we will make America great again. Thank you. God bless you. And God bless America."[1]

For the other half of Americans, this was a dreadful day. CNN published the hopes and fears (mostly fears) of several citizens on inauguration day. They saw in Trump a strong-armed president; a leader who would be a totalitarian. They compared him with Soviet Russia and Nazi Germany. They were fearful over the future and sad at the passing of Obama.

Presidency Under Pressure

They saw it as the beginning of oppression and the dawn of renewed racism. Xenophobic, racist, anti-Semitic, reality TV, menacing, populist, anti-climate change, anti-LGBT, and authoritarian, were some of the characteristics attributed to Trump. There were protests in Washington D.C. against Trump on inauguration day as well, and 216 were arrested.[2]

Many women felt that the new president did not represent them, and the following day they marched in cities across the country in protest. This protest was especially organized to get the message to the new president that "women's rights are human rights."[3] Protesters considered Trump's platform as one of hate and division, and the rally had several high profile speakers, including Madonna, actresses Ashley Judd and Scarlett Johansson, activists Michael Moore and Gloria Steinem, and Planned Parenthood President Cecile Richards.[4] The press announced that there were more women protesting Trump in the National Mall on Saturday than there had been people at the inauguration on Friday. The war between the new president and the media began immediately. CNN published images and statistics to prove its claim, yet President Trump accused the media of skewing its story to support its own agenda. He said there were a million to a million and a half people there, but the media indicated much fewer. Despite the argument, Trump was at least happy with television viewing at over 30 million, up 11 million from Obama's 2013 inauguration. White House Press Secretary Sean Spicer warned the press to be more responsible and that the president would go directly to the people to keep them informed.[5]

MAKE AMERICA GREAT AGAIN

The new president had a tremendous effect on the stock market. Already, it had previously broken a record with the DOW going over 18,000 points when Trump won the election back in November. But on Inauguration Day, it closed at a new record high near 20,000.[6] Then, just a few days later, on January 25, it broke that record as well. This was attributed to Trump, and the whole scenario was dubbed the "Trump Rally."[7] Those were perceived as booming days and the Trump Rally continued.

One interesting point that made little headlines, but easily noticeable, is Trump's clenched fist, often snapped by photographers. The photographs popped up more and more around election time. It was obvious, yet what was the purpose of publishing these photos rather than others? When watching his speeches, it appears obvious that it is a sign of victory or cheer. Yet, when photographed it seems more like a communist dictator. That was the view apparent after inauguration day, with such images of Trump cropping up in Russia. Would these later be used to show Trump's ties with Russia? In Russia, there was great celebration with the coming of Trump.[8] His presidency did not necessarily change anything, yet, when he spoke with Russian President Putin on January 29, there appeared to be a friendly exchange between the two leaders.[9] Within a couple weeks, more controversy cropped up over Russia and Trump with national security adviser Michael Flynn resigning because he had withheld information about his talks with Russia in December 2016. Flynn said that he did not discuss lifting sanctions with the Russian ambassador, yet it appeared that he had. This caused yet another battle between the press and the president, since it involved leaked intel, published in the

Presidency Under Pressure

press.[10] It was later discovered that Flynn accepted payments for lobby appearances before Russian organizations. The Flynn problem would soon become a big deal.[11]

Israel was another country to make headlines as friendly towards Trump. Leaders in Israel were happy about Trump's new position as president. Israeli Prime Minister Benjamin Netanyahu accepted an invitation from Trump to come to the US the following month to discuss the relationship between the two countries. Prominent among the discussions would likely be the issue of Israeli settlements.[12] In the days leading up to the meeting, the White House made a statement saying that Trump did not support *new* settlements since that seemed like an impediment to peace.[13]

Back home, Trump's business continued to function as before, after assuming office. Almost humorous was a new swipe at him. A watch dog group began a lawsuit accusing him of receiving money from foreign businesses – wherein they paid to stay at his hotels.[14] Another issue faced by the president was the demand for him to release his tax returns. 214,000 signatures were collected to demand a response from the White House. Senior advisor Kellyanne Conway said the response was that Trump would not release them. This seemed to contradict the old promise that Trump would release them after an audit was finished. Conway insisted that people "don't care" about the returns anyway and that they care more about the betterment of their own finances than knowing about Trump's situation. Nevertheless, CBS reported on a poll that showed 74% of American's wanting them to be released.[15]

MAKE AMERICA GREAT AGAIN

There were also discussions about Trump's allegations of voter fraud that continued as they had before elections. The media repeated that the claim was debunked, but Trump continued to say how he would have won the popular election if it had not been for 3 to 5 million illegal immigrants who voted for Clinton. When asked about it, house press secretary Sean Spicer said the White House might even consider an investigation into voter fraud.[16] Then, President Trump himself tweeted, "I will be asking for a major investigation into VOTER FRAUD, including those registered to vote in two states, those who are illegal and ... even, those registered to vote who are dead (and many for a long time). Depending on results, we will strengthen up voting procedures!" The media continued to be critical.[17] The Huffington Post called Trump a liar for saying that there was fraud.[18]

Trump passed several executive orders during his first few days as president. The first came on inauguration day with a jab at Obamacare. Its purpose was to "exercise all authority and discretion available to them to waive, defer, grant exemptions from, or delay" financial burdens due to the law upon American citizens. Forbes explained how this would "severely damage" Obamacare.[19] The following Monday, Trump withdrew the US from the Trans Pacific Partnership, reinstated the Mexico City Policy that limited abortion access from federally funded NGOs, and finally, he froze federal workforce hiring. These executive orders proved that he meant business and would keep campaign promises. Trump hoped to better the American working class by withdrawing from the TPP. The Mexico City Policy change was not a surprise, since that rule had changed with

Presidency Under Pressure

every president since Reagan.[20] Nevertheless, it signaled a shift toward right-to-life, and when Mike Pence became the first vice-president to speak to the Right For Life march in Washington D.C. the transition was apparent. He told them "It's a good day for life," praising Trump as a president who would "proudly stand for the right to life."[21]

Trump also revived the doomed Keystone XL pipeline which Obama had sidelined in 2015 and promoted the Dakota Access pipeline which had stalled in the last days of Obama's presidency. The new president was certainly making a splash with so many speedy changes.[22] Fortune published an article criticizing the decisions, saying that Trump was a bad "deal-maker" due to the action taken.[23]

Another executive order came during the first few days of Trump's presidency. This time it focused on small businesses. The intent was to minimize new regulations and to shrink existing ones. The method was simple: for every new regulation there had to be two regulations removed from existing law. Trump wanted to help the entrepreneurs of the country, saying "The American dream is back, and we're going to create an environment for small business like we haven't had in many, many decades."[24]

President Trump hit the ground running after taking office. He used the executive order to make swift changes and implement his policies without obstruction. At least, the executive order normally worked out well as a vehicle of change for the White House, but this president's immigration policy would soon run into a wall in the form of the supreme court.

CHAPTER VIII
Keeping the Bad Dudes Out

TRUMP'S cabinet nominees faced renewed scrutiny as confirmation hearings approached. The press speculated on the chances of Rex Tillerson's confirmation as Secretary of State. Would Marco Rubio oppose him? Sens. John McCain and Lindsey O. Graham had decided to support him though, so Tillerson appeared to have growing support.[1] Perhaps the least support went to Betsy DeVos, the nominee for education secretary. By February 1, her chances of confirmation seemed slim.[2] In fact, it was reported that "virtually all" Democrat senators would vote against several of Trump's cabinet picks.[3] This doesn't mean that all Democrats thought the choices were all that bad. In fact, one Democrat apparently told Trump that Attorney General nominee Sen. Jeff Sessions was a fantastic man and a great friend, but he for "political reasons" he could not vote for him.[4] The trouble between Trump and those who opposed him was just beginning.

On the Wednesday following inauguration, Trump signed a law to build the wall at the American-Mexican border and to "beef up the nation's deportation force." For him, this was only the fulfilment of campaign promises, but he was criticized for it. Mexican President Mr. Peña Nieto responded that he may not come to visit the US because of it.[5] Trump insisted that Mexico would pay for the construction of the wall, but Mexico insisted that it would not. The next day, Peña Nieto cancelled the upcoming visit

PRESIDENCY UNDER PRESSURE

with President Trump.[6] They spoke a few days later, but with no agreement about the wall. Trump's action against illegal immigrants included withholding federal money from "sanctuary cities" shielding them from deportation.[7] Around the same time, Trump also spoke with Australian Prime Minister Malcolm Turnbull. Leaks from Trump's conversations with the leaders of Mexico and Australia became public, showing tension between them and Trump. With Australia, it arose from a deal previously made by President Obama by which refugees detained in that country would make their way to the US. This did not go over well with Trump, who allegedly hung up on the Prime Minister.[8]

Then, two days later came the bombshell executive order suspending immigration and refugees. Trump indefinitely suspended Syrian refugees, and suspended for 120 days the entire refugee program. Furthermore, he suspended for 90 days immigration from countries with "ties to terror," including Syria, Yemen, Sudan, Somalia, Iraq, Iran and Libya. The intent was to step back and form a better vetting process and thus curb terrorism so that Americans could be sure that radical Muslims would not come into the country. However, the plan favored persecuted Christians in Muslim countries by prioritizing their possibility to immigrate into the US. The criticism was immediate.[9] Thousands of protesters took to the streets during the following days. Airports across the US were filled with people holding signs of protest over the 100-200 people being detained from entering the US. A judge in Brooklyn immediately took action to suspend the order.[10] Over the next three days the media blasted the decision, calling it a Muslim ban. Trump responded by saying that it was not about religion, but about

KEEPING THE BAD DUDES OUT

terrorism and protecting the country. But even Senator Mitch McConnell said, "the United States should not implement a religious test."[11] On the other hand, conservatives countered that the countries on the travel ban had actually been compiled by Obama.[12] Nonetheless, through a spokesperson, Obama condemned the action and voiced his support for the protesters. Acting Attorney General Sally Yates did not support the ban, and Trump immediately fired her, bringing in someone who would support him.[13] While everyone seemed to be calling it a "ban," Sean Spicer said it was not a ban, while Trump simply said that people can call it whatever they want, but the intent was to keep the "bad dudes" out of the US.[14]

Even as president elect, Trump faced riots. Now that he was president the question arose: how will he deal with them? One possibility of action came after a protest at University of California Berkeley with about 1500 protesters hurling smoke bombs, breaking windows and starting a bonfire in a successful effort to cancel a talk given by Breitbart News editor Milo Yiannopoulos. Trump's response: "If U.C. Berkeley does not allow free speech and practices violence on innocent people with a different point of view - NO FEDERAL FUNDS?"[15]

Why the opposition to Trump? Was he moving too quickly? He had, after all, promised to get things done if elected. Now he prided himself to sticking to campaign promises. Press secretary Sean Spicer boasted that within the first few weeks, "The administration has already racked up more than 60 significant actions...[including] 21 executive actions, 16 meetings with foreign leaders and 10 stakeholder meetings." But according to a Gallup poll, this was too fast for most Americans, although it seems that the majority of most of the unhappy people were Democrats.[16]

For the Trumps, the whole presidential thing was new. Now, anything that might have been private or public all of a sudden became bigger news than it had been before. The mockery of Trump at Saturday Night Live continued without end. As one media outlet put it, SNL was almost purposely putting on skits that were "reverse-engineered from things that would enrage Donald Trump. And what could be more enraging to a man as sexist, racist, and TV-obsessed as Trump than being played by a black woman on television." This was a break from Alec Baldwin's standard impression of Trump.[17]

The First Lady, Melania, was also prominent in the media. She filed a libel suit with a tabloid for making allegations that she used to work with an escort company in the 1990s, saying that it hurt her business opportunities. The media questioned her intentions, believing that she was mixing her new position as First Lady and business. Did she have something to gain in business due to her new position? Was she exploiting her position? Regardless of the answer, in due course she won the lawsuit for an undisclosed amount, but possibly around the $150-million originally demanded.[18]

Even Trump's daughter Ivanka ran into trouble when Nordstrom dropped her line of clothing and accessories. The president blasted them for it, saying that his daughter was being treated "unfairly." The New York Times reported that this raised "ethical questions" about him mixing his personal

KEEPING THE BAD DUDES OUT

business with his role as president.[19] In fact, Kellyanne Conway took even more heat for her comments on Fox News about Ivanka's products, since Conway's words were seen as a "free commercial." In fact, Conway was investigated but was only accused of "inadvertently" promoting the clothing line, even though some people thought she had seriously violated ethics.[20] Conway was becoming unpopular with the media. She also lost credibility for not being "in the know" about the facts surrounding the Trump presidency. After all of this, MSNBC's "Morning Joe" said she was no longer welcome on the show due to this reason.[21]

Possible choices for Supreme Court pick came up during this time. Apparently Trump had narrowed it down to three: Neil Gorsuch, from the federal appeals court in Denver, William H. Pryor Jr., from the 11th Circuit Court of Appeals, and Thomas Hardiman from the 3rd Circuit Court of Appeals. The latter was supposed to be his ultimate pick, but sources said to be on guard as Trump could surprise everyone.[22] TIME reported that top Democrat Senator Church Schumer promised to block any nominee for Supreme Court who was not "mainstream." So, there was little if any support from the left in Trump's choices.[23]

The nomination for Supreme Court finally came on January 31, with Trump honing in on Neil Gorsuch. Of him, the president said, "Judge Gorsuch has a superb intellect, an unparalleled legal education, and a commitment to interpreting the Constitution according to its text. He will make an incredible justice as soon as the Senate confirms him" – just the kind of fellow the Republicans were looking

Presidency Under Pressure

for. Mitch McConnell praised him, as did House Speaker Paul Ryan. Their Democratic counterparts, Chuck Schumer and Nancy Pelosi were not thrilled about the selection, implying that Gorsuch was out of step with the times, and far too constitutional and conservative.[24] Chances were, Democrats would attempt to filibuster the choice. If they did, Trump had some advice for McConnell: "If you can, Mitch, go nuclear," meaning the Republicans force the decision by a numerical majority.[25]

With the pick of Supreme Court on its way, Trump ran into a serious roadblock with his immigration order. After Washington and Minnesota filed lawsuits against the refugee suspension, a federal judge in Seattle placed a restraining order on it on the first Friday in February, effectively halting the order nationwide.[26] Within a few hours, travelers from the banned countries were flying into the United States again. This resulted in stinging remarks from the Trump Administration. It was called outrageous and ridiculous. Trump said that the "so called judge" was essentially taking law-enforcement "away from our country."[27] He did not waste time, and the next day the Department of Justice filed an appeal to overturn the ruling, but it was denied the following day.[28]

Trump's blast at the "so called judge" immediately produced speculation on whether or not the pick for Supreme Court would be independent of Trump, although he was "handpicked."[29] This would now impact Gorsuch's hearing. The latter responded to Trump's remarks, saying they were "disheartening" and "demoralizing." Perhaps these words proved him capable of remaining independent.[30]

KEEPING THE BAD DUDES OUT

As the first weeks of February passed, the battle with the 9th court circuit continued. It now looked into whether or not Trump's ban was really an anti-Muslim law, but the suspension of Trump's order remained intact.[31] The president did not give up though. He continued his twitter attacks on the judges for blocking his order. He was confident, saying, "We'll win that battle, but we also have a lot of other options, including just filing a brand-new order,"[32] Rather than taking it to a higher court right away, which might set an unappealing precedence, Trump sent the case back to the 9th circuit to have another hearing with 10-11 judges rather than the original 3. Perhaps he could now be successful.[33]

Other headlines rose and fell in the midst of the 9th circuit situation. Gen. Mattis made a statement saying that the American people had paid too much of NATO's costs for too long. It was time for other members to begin paying to defend "Western values." Europeans were unhappy with the decision, although the UK agreed with the US.[34]

At the same time, Trump's cabinet picks had their hearings – both with difficulty and with ease. Andrew Puzder had been chosen for labor secretary, yet his reputation floundered as stories of his divorce from 25 years before spread around. Then, it came out that he had employed an illegal immigrant in his home at one time. Amid this, he withdrew his bid for the position, so Trump now chose Alexander Acosta, who had at least had some public service experience under President Bush. But now the Democrats vowed to scrutinize this pick as well.[35] On the other hand, others were confirmed. Rep. Mick Mulvaney

PRESIDENCY UNDER PRESSURE

became Trump's budget chief although only by a two-vote majority. Senator McCain was against the budget chief choice.[36] Former Texas governor Rick Perry was handily confirmed 62 to 37 as energy secretary.[37]

At least some of Trump's cabinet picks were confirmed with ease. This, however, was in stark contrast to the difficulties the president faced. Obviously, the President Trump did not have the sweeping success in immigration reform that he hoped to have. Now if he could just get Neil Gorsuch confirmed as a supreme court justice, then he would have one major success under his belt.

CHAPTER IX
Address to the Nation

EVER since the pre-inauguration press conference, President Trump's relationship with the media was unstable. Now it seemed the norm that Trump to criticize the media at these events, so when he held another press conference in mid-February, the president made clear his ideas on the matter saying, "the press has become so dishonest that if we don't talk about it, we are doing a tremendous disservice to the American people. The press is out of control, the level of dishonesty is out of control." He felt it his duty to inform the public about the bad stories out there. He said that his administration was working like a fine-tuned machine, yet "I turn on the TV and open the newspaper and sees stories of chaos. Chaos."[1] And realistically, anyone looking at the news would concur that the stories were almost literally all negative. Trump attributed this to the fact that he was carrying out his campaign promises and the liberal media did not like this. The Washington Post's article on the scenario was rather humorous to read, since they had to agree that trust in the media was at an all-time low. Yet, the writer believed that Trump's goal was to withdraw attention from himself, "changing the subject from Russia and Mike Flynn."[2]

Afterwards, Trump held a campaign type rally in Florida, where he told supporters he could speak directly to them "without the filter of the fake news."[3] The war with the media escalated. The Washington Post reported that he

PRESIDENCY UNDER PRESSURE

called the media "the enemy of the American People!"[4] For the casual news reader, this appeared as fact. NPR reported the same: "Trump called the press the 'enemy of the American people,' in a tweet recently."[5] Yet, when speaking at the Conservative Political Action Conference, the president used even this quote as proof of fake news, saying, "The dishonest media did not explain that I called the fake news the enemy of the people. The fake news. They dropped off the word 'fake.' And all of a sudden the story became the media is the enemy." The Washington Post attempted to back up its story by providing the actual tweet which listed several big news organizations as sources of fake news and concluding: "By listing major media organizations as the enemy, Trump was clearly making a statement about the broader news media." This was a fine example of the media war. Trump said something and the media made a conclusion.[6]

For Trump supporters, while the media focused on the negative aspects of Trump's presidency, they wondered why he could not be praised for progress being made towards campaign promises. For those who did not support the president, he was a symbol of division and hatred, promoting hatred in the nation. It was true that finding something positive in the media about Trump was nearly impossible, although Trump did say things that were vague, just as others might do if they did not use teleprompters. His comment about the bad things happening in Sweden due to immigration caused an uproar, but afterwards he clarified that he got his information from Fox News.[7] It was interesting how omnipresent Trump was in the media. One New York Times writer attempted to take a week-long break

ADDRESS TO THE NATION

from "Trump news" but found it impossible to do so. The president was everywhere and part of nearly every event reported on in the nation. The writer blamed this partially on social media which tended to exaggerate anything "Trump."[8] Certainly, Trump seemed to use the media for his own ends. The media claimed that his goal was the promotion of Trump himself, whereas Trump said it was for the American people.[9] Perhaps a gesture of goodwill was needed and for that Trump promised to give his $400,000 salary as president towards charity but asked the press to help him decided where to donate it.[10]

The president had his fair share of opposition. Billionaire Tom Steyer put his words and wallet against him and got vocal about it, saying, "I see this election as ushering in an administration that is waging an all-out attack on American interests, on the civil liberties of Americans, and on the American people in general."[11] He had heartily supported Obama, but not the new president. Michael Moore, a professional social activist was of the same opinion and even organized a website to promote "every upcoming action, protest, march, sit-in, town hall, anti-Trump, pro-democracy event in all 50 states!"[12] Actors continued to voice their opposition as well. George Clooney said Trump was a demagogue, and reportedly "slammed" Trump in an interview. Ben Affleck seconded these sentiments.[13]

In the meantime, amidst the controversies, Trump pushed ahead with his program. He planned spending cuts to reduce the national debt, the replacement for Obamacare, and tax reform as his first speech to Congress approached. He promised Americans that the government under his

Presidency Under Pressure

leadership would not waste their money. Nonetheless, the media reported that Trump was going to spend lots of money on the border wall, infrastructure, and the military.[14] This was true. For example, Trump planned "sharp increases" in military spending. On the other hand, he was going to cut billions of dollars spent by the EPA and possibly 20% of its personnel.[15] As for Obamacare, Trump found that repealing it or overhauling it was an "unbelievably complex subject."[16]

In addition to financial changes, the president also decided to get involved with transgender use of bathrooms. He rescinded Obama rules which allowed them to use the bathroom that coincided with their gender identity. Thus, he took a conservative line, even though his education secretary opposed the action. It was reported that Attorney General Jeff Sessions was responsible for pushing the president to remove the rule.[17] The bathroom was not the only place Trump took action, he also took an axe to Obama's environmental work by removing restrictions on coal mines from "freely dumping tons of debris into the streams and mountain hollows of America's mining communities."[18] With all the destruction to Obama's legacy, it would not have been surprising to find Obama entering politics immediately after leaving office, and it appeared that he might. At least, that is what former US Attorney General Eric Holder told the media. Trump also asked for the resignation of 46 U.S. attorneys who were carryovers from the Obama Administration. While this was a relatively normal occurrence, it received headlines when one of them refused to do so and was fired.[19]

ADDRESS TO THE NATION

These happenings were things that conservatives supported and had hoped to find in a president. Thus, it came as little surprise that Trump spoke at the Conservative Political Action Committee (CPAC) in late February, confirming campaign promises and affirming swift action taken in a conservative direction. Not surprisingly, his speech was fact-checked by the media.[20] This became common. For example, when the president and first lady hosted a dinner for the governors of states, Trump mused that he heard it was a record that 46 governors came to the dinner. Trump was always looking for a record, but the media was always investigating his words – reporters probably hoped to find that he was wrong again.[21] In fact, the tension between the media and president escalated. For the first time in 36 years a president did not attend the annual White House Correspondents' dinner. Two explanations came from the White House: "This wasn't a president that was elected to spend his time with reporters and celebrities," and "it's kind of naive of us to think that we can all walk into a room for a couple of hours and pretend that some of that tension isn't there." The Correspondents Association responded that it would uphold First Amendment rights.[22] Trump also had an unpleasant experience at the dinner when he previously attended in 2011. President Obama roasted him for questioning his birth as a US citizen.

Then came one bright episode in the early presidency. Just days after CPAC, President Trump gave his first address to the Nation before Congress. He outlined his goals and hopes. Immigration reform, tax reform, job growth, protection and support for Americans, healthcare, infrastructure, and the military were included in his speech.

PRESIDENCY UNDER PRESSURE

Republicans were proud of him. Democrats were not so happy about it. Yet, Trump told them to unite for the good of the nation. The New York Times reported that while Trump had been rapidly ramrodding his agenda via executive orders, this was now "an attempt to open a new phase and reflected his need for cooperation from Congress."[23] The Washington Post followed up with fact-checking just as it did to Trump's CPAC speech, saying that it was filled with "many of the president's false claims are old favorites that he trots out on a regular, almost daily basis."[24] NPR, however, had a positive outlook on the speech that might have a balming effect on politics surrounding the president. Certainly, the most touching part of the speech was when he acknowledged Carryn Owens, the widow of Navy SEAL William "Ryan" Owens. She received a sustained ovation.[25]

Many hoped that the address would boost Trump's approval ratings among Democrats. He was, after all, reaching out to them. He needed their help. His ratings one month into presidency were the lowest ever recorded by Gallup since it began polling in 1953.[26] Even former president George W. Bush gave his "tacit criticism" of the new president.[27] Business, however, seemed to approve of the message since the DOW broke 21,000 for the first time afterwards – another record under Trump's belt. One chief investment officer explained it like this: "President Trump came out and gave a presidential speech, which reassured a lot of people who questioned whether his administration would reach normality,"[28]

But normality was not a hallmark of the Trump administration. Immediately following these events, a new

ADDRESS TO THE NATION

controversy arose with the revelation that Attorney General Jeff Sessions had spoken with the Russian ambassador twice during the Trump campaign the previous year. Michael Flynn had just resigned over a similar accusation. Now it seemed that round two was approaching. Chuck Schumer led Democrats in calling for Sessions to resign. At the very least, even some Republicans thought he should recuse himself from the investigation into Russian meddling with the US elections. Yet, Trump said that Sessions had his total confidence.[29]

This was nothing new. It was only the continuation of the whole complaint that Trump and Russia were connected and that the latter helped him win the election. It seemed that the Obama administration had even sought out information connecting the two, that is, the media claimed that Obama officials "scrambled to spread information" about the connection prior to him leaving office.[30] One thing that came out in a CNN interview, but not widely-spread across the media, was a comment by a top Russian official who acknowledged that "People associated with Hillary Clinton's campaign also met with Russian ambassador Sergey Kislyak."[31] Apparently meetings were normal, so why all the hype about Trump?

Sessions soon recused himself when the situation became more heated. Apparently, Trump was furious over this action and said that the attorney general should not have recused himself. Nonetheless, now instead of Sessions, his new deputy would oversee any investigations into the 2016 campaign.[32] The Flynn/Sessions connection with Russia was all across the news.

Presidency Under Pressure

Then, over the following weekend, Trump tweeted a serious accusation towards his predecessor. He said that he just found out that Obama had tapped Trump tower in October, just before the elections. Immediately the press was swirling with this story. Sessions was all but forgotten. Was that Trump's intention? His critics thought so. Nancy Pelosi believed this, and the Washington Post printed a whole article outlining why this was so. Did it work? Yes. Obama's spokesman denied the surveillance. Nevertheless, Trump requested an investigation into the matter. One indirect effect was a drop in the stock market. It also reportedly had a negative impact of American-Russian relations. CNN wrote that the connections between Trump's people and Russians were "threatening to overshadow his political agenda."[33] The revelation certainly caused a wave of controversy as top Republicans and Obama cast doubt on it. The latter was reportedly "furious" over it.[34] Thus, President Trump ignited another controversial situation which would engulf the media over the following days.

CHAPTER X
Trials and Errors

IN the midst of other ongoing circumstances, Trump issued his revised "travel ban" executive order in early March. This one allowed those with visas from "six majority-Muslim nations" to travel to the US, but banned the issuance of new visas for 90 days. Iraq was removed from the ban. It also reduced the total allowance of refugees down to 50,000 from 110,000 and established a 120 day ban on refugees from entering the US. These and other points of the ban still angered the same people who opposed the previous ban. It was, however, more concise than before and allowed greater freedom for those who were already in the US.[1] Nonetheless, Hawaii promised to combat the order and a federal judge there would hear the lawsuit on the day before it was supposed to become law.[2] Other states got involved, and pretty soon there were over a half dozen opposed to the order. Then, just when it was supposed to become law, Hawaii blocked the order, indicating that it was anti-Muslim, and could also hurt the state's tourist economy. A Maryland judge also blocked it. Those who opposed Trump said that he really intended a Muslim ban as he had speculated during the election campaign. In Virginia, however, a federal judge sided with Trump. The supreme court had once again trumped The Donald.[3]

The Obamacare replacement came in early March. Senator Rand Paul called it "Obamacare lite" and others called it Obamacare 2.0. Basically, the conservatives did not agree with its measures. Especially at question was the part of it that expanded Medicaid. Other than that, it ended the penalty of Obamacare 1.0, while allowing insurance companies to charge a 30% fee if someone allowed their insurance to lapse. Other than the conservative and moderates who rejected it, other Republicans supported it, including House Speaker Paul Ryan. President Trump threw his weight behind it.[4] Despite some support, the effort looked doomed. The problem seemed to be Trump's efforts to appease everyone, and he was running into the same situation in trying to keep funding Planned Parenthood while making it unable to provide for abortions.[5] Some GOP leaders thought Obamacare should be left on its own to self-destruct. Yet, Trump was confident that his new plan would drive down insurance costs significantly. Everyone awaited the Congressional Budget Office report to see just where the cost would be and how many people might lose coverage under the new system.[6] When it finally did come, the numbers did not look good. According to it, 24 million people would lose health coverage by 2026, if Obamacare was repealed. Republicans immediately looked for ways to fine tune the replacement. Trump said that this was expected. Negotiation was, after all, his specialty.[7]

The problem with healthcare, however, would not go away. Conservative Republicans would not unite with Trump even though he threatened that they could lose midterm elections if they did not repeal Obamacare via his proposal. Despite the threat, CNN reported that the president was willing to appease the right and alter the healthcare bill, thus making it more conservative. House speaker Paul Ryan was on board and pushed to get votes in favor as is. Trump's

TRIALS AND ERRORS

first major test as a negotiator was in full swing! Nonetheless, no agreement was reached by the time the voting was to occur, so supporters decided to delay voting in an effort to gain support from conservatives in Congress. Democrats on the other hand were not going to support it anyway. The final decision would come a few days later.[8]

Meanwhile, the Justice Department was supposed to turn over evidence of Obama's alleged tapping of Trump to the House Intelligence Committee by March 13.[9] Did it really happen? No one really thought so. But Trump did say that more interesting information would soon come out about the subject. But what did he really say when first bringing the issue up? He didn't say that Obama was tapping him, but that he had heard about it.[10] So was this just another case of the Salena Zito rule? The latter came up with the intriguing point that Trump supporters took him "seriously, but not literally," but the press took him "literally, but not seriously."[11] At any rate, when the report came out that the congressional committee had not found any evidence of tapping Trump Tower it was not surprising.[12] FBI Director James Comey said there was no evidence. Yet Trump pushed on the fight with the media. Sean Spicer claimed that media coverage of the Trump tapping was unfair. As the Washington Post reported, he said that "the press was being much more skeptical of Trump's wiretapping claim than it has been of allegations that Trump colluded with Russia — despite there being no definitive proof of either." But to that newspaper, these were incomparable, since "the White House doesn't seem to understand the difference between a circumstantial case and a conspiracy theory." But conservatives pushed the point that there was not a shred of

Presidency Under Pressure

evidence that Trump's team colluded with Russia during the elections, so why push that throughout the media?[13]

On the other hand, there were some unusual connections, or disconnections, which begged questions. Secretary of State Tillerson declined to go to a leaders' meeting with NATO and instead scheduled to meet with the president of China and then go on to visit Russia. NATO, of course, was quite unhappy with the decision. So, either the complaining brought results, or a solution was already at hand, since President Trump decided to meet NATO himself.[14]

As viewed in the media, it seemed that the majority of Americans were dissatisfied with Trump. Take the environmentalists. They believed Trump to be tearing up Obama's triumphs in that field, so they brought their message and rakes to the battle and carved "NO MORE TIGERS, NO MORE WOODS" into one of Trump's golf courses in California.[15] One artist in Arizona portrayed disapproval of Trump on a billboard with atomic bombs going off and dollar signs in the form of swastikas. According to Gallup, Trump's approval rating plummeted, and on March 18 only 37% of Americans believed he was doing a good job – the worst approval rating since Gallop first polled president approval in 1945. Obama was at 60% at the same time during his presidency. The Wall Street Journal said that Trump probably saw this as "fake news," while claiming that most Americans saw him as a "fake president."[16] This all led Monmouth University to run a poll to investigate Trump's attacks on the media. They found that most receivers of news trusted ABC News, Fox News, and

TRIALS AND ERRORS

MSNBC more than they trusted Trump, while recognizing that the media gets into "fake news" once in a while.[17]

But what was fake about Trump? Was he dishonest? Did he keep his word? Well, he never released his tax returns for one. The issue of the president's tax returns came back to life with a MSNBC story publicizing Trump's 1040 return from 2005. The reporter claimed to have found the return "in the mail." For this unlikely story, Trump once again leveled the fake news charge at the organization.[18] Nonetheless, it showed that Trump payed $38 million in taxes, debunking the idea that he did not pay taxes.

Other parts of Trump's private life moved into the presidency. Ivanka also reentered the media with a start in March when she was given security clearance and an office in the West Wing of the White House. When elected, Trump had said she would not get an office there. While her husband held an official role as advisor, her role was unofficial. This led people to question the ethics of moving her into such a position. In fact, she was present in many significant meetings between the president and foreign leaders. Was Trump practicing nepotism? Should she have been there? For many, this new situation posed serious questions and only proved the terrors of a Trump presidency.[19] So much flak came from this new situation that Ivanka found it necessary to become an employee of the White House in order to be bound by ethics laws. She did not receive a salary in her new role, but now she was an official advisor of the president.[20]

Yet, Trump defended himself every step of the way. When attacked, he attacked back. Even if the media could

Presidency Under Pressure

prove he was wrong, he would come back to show how he was actually in the right. What would he do with future confrontations? For instance, a former "The Apprentice" contestant pursued pressing charges against the president for alleged sexual harassment. Trump would probably just fight back and claim falsity as before.[21]

Intrigue further developed with the placement of Jared Kushner, Ivanka's husband, as a senior advisor to the president. Subsequently, the son-in-law took on quasi secretary of state activities such as visiting Iraq. The media questioned this development and contrasted it with Stephen Bannon's apparent decrease in favor as Trump's Chief Strategist. After all, the latter was removed from the National Security Council, though for reasons which seemed vague at the time. Was it voluntary, or did it signify a falling out? Time would tell.[22] Despite questioning his ability to fulfil the role given to him, Kushner as a choice to visit the Middle East was not necessarily an arbitrary one, since his family had close ties with Israel and he was a deeply religious Orthodox Jew.[23]

All of these things were the continuation of the numerous Trump stories. The confirmation hearings of Neil Gorsuch for Supreme Court justice came to the forefront of news towards the end of March. Apparently, he prepared for it with mock hearings, visiting senators, and reviewing in detail his own track record. It would be tough, but everyone, including his critics, agreed about his calm, humble, and agreeable character. That, however, did not protect him from a difficult hearing. It ranged from his opinion on the president, to transgender issues, to his previous opinions among other things. When pressed by Democrats, he worked around answering important questions on gun rights, abortion, assisted suicide. At any rate, he assured listeners that he would act independently and not make decisions based on his own personal opinions.[24]

As far as Democrats were concerned, Gorsuch failed to win them over, and they vowed, with Schumer at the helm, to resist his nomination and filibuster his appointment. The vote would come in April, and the Republicans were prepared to use the "nuclear" option if necessary to win Gorsuch's nomination to the court.[25] In Gorsuch Trump would have what Democrats were calling his single major victory of the first 100 days.

CHAPTER XI
Go Nuclear

ALONG with the Supreme Court nomination came the continuation of the repeal and replacement of Obamacare. President Trump was trying to work with the Freedom Caucus to get conservative support, but was unsuccessful. He really needed them, but despite the lack of full Republican support, Trump decided to move ahead and push a vote in Congress on March 24. Predictably, it failed. So, Trump said he was done with healthcare and would move on to tax reform. There was a problem though – the two were closely connected. The president blamed Democrats for the failure. Although Trump would not blame House Speaker Ryan, the Washington Post wrote that the latter "remains without a signature accomplishment as speaker, and the defeat undermines Trump's image as a skilled dealmaker willing to strike compromises to push his agenda forward."[1]

The healthcare bill failure also cast doubt on the future ability of Republicans to work together in other situations. Take the budget for instance. Would they be able to agree in that regard? Would conservatives try to defund Planned Parenthood and cause a government shutdown? Would Democrats support a Republican led budget? These were questions spreading around in the post-repeal-Obamacare climate. Trump told the Freedom Caucus to get on board soon, or they might lose in 2018 elections. In fact, he singled out Michigan Rep. Justin Amash, saying that the

Presidency Under Pressure

representative should be defeated in the primaries by a not so conservative Republican.[2]

If conservatives were unhappy with Trump's healthcare proposal, they hailed his rollback on Obama's climate change policies. He was flanked by miners as he signed the new executive order. This was to bring jobs to the US and unravel EPA restrictions that prevented the coal industry from continuing as before. While not withdrawing immediately from the Paris Agreement by which Obama had bound the US to reduce greenhouse gas emissions, the executive order ended the actions taken by the US towards that end. Other countries were shocked at the reversal and hoped that other important participants such as China and Brazil would not follow suit. France, on the other hand, boasted that there were many other nations who would fill the vacuum left by "Mr. Trump's short-termism."[3]

The issue of Russia refused to let go as Trump's 100 days rolled on. The Washington Post said that Trump was struggling to get out of the controversy. Then, the president got his first big break with regards Obama's surveillance of Trump during the election campaign. Susan Rice, a national security adviser under Obama, admitted that the Trump team had in fact been surveilled even up to a year before the election. Apparently, this was done in connection with Russia's involvement in the election process. But, Trump saw this as vindication saying, "Such amazing reporting on unmasking and the crooked scheme against us by @foxandfriends. 'Spied on before nomination.' The real story."[4] Additionally, the news broke that the FBI had obtained a FISA warrant in summer of 2016 to investigate

Go Nuclear

Carter Page, a foreign policy advisor to the Trump team. Allegedly, Page was acting as an agent for Russia. Trump said he never met him, although Page was remotely involved in the campaign.[5] This story stretched into late spring when Fox News published an article detailing Page's denial of claiming to be an advisor to Trump and instead blaming the "mainstream media and the 'corrupt Clinton regime' – not himself – for repeatedly saying he was an adviser to the Donald Trump presidential team." Even the president's lawyer wrote to Page saying that he was not an advisor in any way to Trump.[6]

In early April, the Senate voted on Neil Gorsuch for Supreme Court. As expected, Republicans failed to get the support they needed for the necessary 60 votes. Then came the Democratic filibuster. When he nominated Gorsuch, the president had suggested going "nuclear" and that is exactly what happened. Therefore, the Republicans changed Senate precedence and voted to allow a simple majority to confirm the Supreme Court nominee. The Democrats were furious; however, it was they who in 2013 established the nuclear option as a way to get nominees confirmed, albeit not for the Supreme Court. Nonetheless, on April 7 the Republican Party succeeded in confirming Gorsuch – the youngest Supreme Court member ever.[7]

During his campaign, Trump had spoken with authority over how he would deal with Syria and North Korea. Now he had the opportunity to make true his words. Bashar Assad, the leader of Syria, had used chemical weapons on the Syrian people, and Trump vowed that this would not be ignored. More than 80 people died, including women and children. Secretary of State Rex Tillerson announced, "It's a serious matter, it requires a serious response."[8] And that serious response came in the form of a volley of Tomahawk missiles fired by the US at the airbase from which the chemical attack seemingly originated. Russia and Iran objected to the intervention saying that an investigation should be done to find out more about Assad's use of chemical weapons. Was America seeking a regime change or could it work this out diplomatically? It was not wholly clear. The Russians supported Assad and said rebels were responsible. Yet, the US said that Russia was trying to cover up the truth. Meanwhile, the Chinese encouraged a political solution while condemning the use of chemical weapons.[9]

Tensions also arose between North Korea and the US. The small country continued to test missiles and make threatening comments about its nuclear capabilities. So, to prove his intention to do something about Kim Jong-Un, Trump deployed the USS Carl Vinson to the area saying that, if necessary, the US would independently take on North Korea on its own, adding that it would be best if China dealt with the nearby country first. Also, it seemed that Trump put trade relations on the line in an effort to get China to take action; and on the outside, it seemed that the Chinese did not do much.[10] Nonetheless, Trump continued to communicate with their president, as well as the leader of Japan. The three countries appeared to be working together as Kim Jong-Un's government rattled threats to destroy an American military base in South Korea. Meanwhile, Vice-President Mike Pence made the journey to Asia, smoothing the US relationship with other countries in that region, including a visit to South Korea. The situation tensed as the president called a top-

GO NUCLEAR

secret meeting at the White House with 100 senators, but the exact purpose of the meeting was unclear to the public.[11]

Intertwined with international woes came the promised Trump budget. With it, Trump's hiring freeze for government jobs came to an end, but the budget plan ordered cuts to various parts of the government, including the EPA. The Trump administration said this was a "big part of draining the swamp." The budget was supposed to trim government to make it more businesslike.[12] But it was deeply connected with other campaign promises such as building the wall on the Mexico-US border and tax reform. The wall had to be paid for, and it was beginning to appear that Mexico would not pay for it, although Trump had promised during the campaign that it would. Nancy Pelosi called it "immoral" and "expensive." Would Trump get the support he needed to finance the wall?[13] As the time for voting on government funding neared, Trump held firm on the necessity of funding the wall with a government spending bill. But Democrats certainly did not support it. On the other hand, Trump did not want the government to shut down.[14] His campaign promise teetered on the edge of collapse. "Mexico won't pay for it. Democrats hate it. Border-state Republicans don't like it. Congressional GOP leaders would rather not undertake it. There could be an avoidable government shutdown over it." So began a Washington Post article on the subject. But the approaching possibility of a shutdown caused the president to back off somewhat and he decided to remove wording in the spending bill which included funding the wall. Though he still intended to build it: "Don't let the fake media tell you that I have changed my position on the WALL. It will get built and help stop drugs, human trafficking etc."[15] He was in a difficult position. Democrats could say he had broken his campaign promise if he made the United States pay for the wall in the spending bill, and they could also say the same thing if Mexico never ended up paying for the wall.

As the president's first 100-day anniversary as president approached, Trump announced some main ideas of his proposed tax plan. Beforehand, the media promised that it would include major tax cuts for corporations and the wealthy, as well as middle class, but cited a Pew study which found that a great deal of Republicans were happy with the taxes they paid and thought that corporations should be taxed more. Furthermore, Democrats were extremely concerned that the wealthy did not pay as much tax as they should. Trump, nevertheless, promised "massive" tax cuts for corporations and individuals. The tax proposals included big breaks for corporations, reducing the tax from 35% to 15%. This would also benefit S corporations, which often were smaller companies with a single owner, but could also be larger ones such as Trump's own business. The proposal would also provide an increase in the deductions claimed when filing taxes.[16]

Not surprisingly, there were those who found Trump's meddling with taxes as self-serving. Opponents still wanted Trump to release his tax returns and on "tax day," April 15, protesters came out across the nation to demand that he do so. However, the president brushed them off saying that the election was over and that they were paid protesters anyway. In Berkeley, California, the protest turned violent when

GO NUCLEAR

Trump supporters held a rally at the same location as tax protesters at the same time.[17]

Meanwhile, the president added to the long list of executive orders, one that altered the way the H1-B visa program worked. Now, instead of companies being able to hire foreign workers by "lottery" selection, they would be required to take the best-qualified for the task. Trump said it put America first and would therefore encourage employment of Americans. The media reminded the public that Trump's vineyard had employed foreign workers under a like program, and therefore he did not practice what he preached.[18] An additional executive order would have withheld money from so-called sanctuary cities that refused to enforce federal immigration laws. But once again, a California supreme court judge blocked it, first temporarily. This was the third executive order blocked during the first 100 days. The president blasted the ruling in several tweets, saying "First the Ninth Circuit rules against the ban & now it hits again on sanctuary cities-both ridiculous rulings. See you in the Supreme Court!" He furthermore accused liberals of "judge shopping."[19] At least if one of these issues ever made it to the highest court in the land, there would be one more conservative judge to hear the case, and it was President Trump who nominated him. Neil Gorsuch thus represented Donald Trump's biggest success yet during the first 100 days.

CHAPTER XII
Tweet the Truth

THAT final week before the 100-day mark was, therefore, eventful. Coincidentally, the budget would also run out on that day unless Congress could unite enough to pass a new budget. At the same time, Trump also sought to successfully find a solution to Obamacare.[20] So now there were two important issues at stake as the deadline approached – the budget, and healthcare. But even in these, Trump appeared to make little progress. In fact, a Washington Post article painted a grim picture of his success during the first 100 days. His only real achievement was the Gorsuch confirmation to the Supreme Court, while at the same time, he remained the "least popular chief executive in modern times" according to the polls.[1]

Trump disagreed, tweeting, "no matter how much I accomplish during the ridiculous standard of the first 100 days, & it has been a lot (including S.C.), media will kill!"[2] The president's relationship with the media and journalists certainly did not improve. In fact, he broke tradition by not attending the annual White House Correspondents' Association dinner on April 29. Instead he decided to hold a rally on that day, since it marked the 100-day milestone. Meanwhile, the dinner proceeded without him with speakers lauding free speech and investigative journalism.[3] They felt threatened by the new president. For example, with all their emphasis on transparency, it really irked them when the Trump administration announced that it would not publish

Presidency Under Pressure

the list of visitors to the White House, marking a "significant shift from the Obama White House."[4]

On the international field things were happening as well. North Korea was just as threatening and testing missiles. The US and China seemed to be working together to denuclearize the Korean peninsula. The US would use force if necessary and China promised to hold to previous U.N. resolutions against nuclear weapons there. Trump was clear that the situation could lead to "major, major conflict" but also reminded everyone that the US would do it alone if necessary. Not that North Korea's missiles were working that well. The May 28 test had failed (as would future missile tests). Nonetheless, the president commented that it "disrespected" China's president. The situation seemed to be quickly escalating.[5]

Also touching upon international relations was the news that Trump was working on an executive order that would remove the US from the North American Free Trade Agreement (NAFTA). That same day, Trump spoke with Canada Prime Minister Justin Trudeau and Mexico President Enrique Peña Nieto and he agreed to renegotiate the trade agreement instead of abolish it. Trump said that withdrawing might "shock the system" which would probably not be a good thing. On the other hand, he reiterated, "if we do not reach a fair deal for all, we will then terminate NAFTA." According to CNN, this was part of a hurried effort by Trump and his advisors "to check off promises made during the campaign" before the 100 days were up.[6]

The final event of the week before reaching that 100th day in office, was for Trump to attend the annual National

Rifle Association convention in Atlanta, Georgia. The New York Times wrote more than one piece on the event. This seemed an unlikely place for an American president to be, especially in light of the previous president's support of gun-control. Acknowledged by Trump, the contrast could not be clearer: "The eight year assault on your Second Amendment freedoms has come to a crashing end...You have a true friend and champion in the White House." He went on to promise never to infringe on the right to keep and bear arms. If the convention hall was filled with thousands of supporters, the president did not find support from others in Congress. Democratic congresswoman from Arizona, Gabby Giffords, who had previously suffered a serious gunshot wound to the head, wanted the president to address the problem of gun violence.[7] A Democrat from Connecticut, Christopher Murphy, also opposed Trump's presence at the convention saying that Trump was there "to celebrate rights of criminals to own guns, to glorify weapons that kill." Murphy then went on to post 11 messages online with the faces of shooting victims. He had been a strong supporter of gun-control, especially since the Sandy Hook Elementary School shooting in Newtown, Conn.[8]

As the 100th day arrived, analysis of President Trump's effectiveness in office began spreading across the media. Stories seemed to prove that the first 100 days were mostly a failure for the new president. Even the last minute week-long spending bill passed by Congress was said to be "more of a defeat for the president than a victory."[9] The list of Trump's failures seemed endless. He was behind in appointments to administration post vacancies. The economy in 2017 was off to a slow start, in fact, it barely grew. Growth was in decline

PRESIDENCY UNDER PRESSURE

and the economy was the slowest it had been in three years. Chuck Schumer criticized Trump's lack of progress.[10] The US-Mexico border wall project had no funding. The Washington Post got ahead of the game to write about Trump's 100 days a couple days before the anniversary. The article said that the steep learning curve for the businessman-turned-president showed through a "mix of signature setbacks and some successes, plus more turmoil than calm emanating from the West Wing of the White House and more division than a coming together in the country." The days, therefore, held a series of efforts by Trump to keep campaign promises and then setbacks such as supreme court judges reversing his immigration bans. Yes, Trump had achieved the confirmation of Neil Gorsuch to the Supreme Court bench, but only by using the "nuclear option." Yet, it had to be admitted that Trump had bipartisan support to conduct strikes on Syria. The Dakota Access pipeline was moving ahead. Obama's environmental regulations were under attack. But the media emphasized the "lack of a singular legislative accomplishment."[11] Fox News called Trump the "disrupter-in-chief" for all of the trouble he caused during the first 100 days in office. The reason? These days were full of constant action which caused "full-on revolts from Democrats in Congress and disparate judges across the country."[12]

On the anniversary of Trump's 100 days in office came the traditional White House Correspondents' Dinner, and he became the first president to miss it since Ronald Reagan in 1981. Instead, the president held a rally with thousands of supporters in Harrisburg, Pennsylvania. Back in Washington D.C., the dinner host, Hasan Minhaj, roasted Trump with various jokes, beginning with: "We've got to address the elephant that's not in the room...The leader of our country is not here. And that's because he lives in Moscow. It's a very long flight. As for the other guy, I think he's in Pennsylvania because he can't take a joke." Meanwhile, Trump criticized the press and voiced his joy at being in Harrisburg with supporters rather than attending the dinner with the dishonest journalists. Trump blasted CNN and MSNBC as "fake news," saying that 89% of their coverage was "purposefully negative." At nearly the same time, Bob Woodward spoke at the dinner saying "the effort today to get this best obtainable version of the truth is largely made in good faith. Mr. President, the media is not 'fake news'." But over in Harrisburg, Trump told his supporters about the above-mentioned networks' "incompetent and dishonest people" and that if the "media's job is to tell the truth, 'the media deserves a very, very big fat failing grade'." The two events thus had two glaringly opposite opinions about the media. Trump concluded that the "dishonest Washington Media is part of the problem, their priorities are not my priorities and they're not your priorities, believe me." The president reminded his audience that he had promised 100 days of action in his inaugural address "and that is what we've delivered."[13]

The New York Times's commemoration of Trump's 100 days commented on the changes that Trump brought to the White House, but also on the presidency's effect on Trump himself. Who could deny the fact that experience alters a person? Mr. Trump had "adapted his approach" when needed, while at the same time doing or saying something on nearly every of the 100 days that "caused presidential

Presidency Under Pressure

historians and seasoned professionals...to use the phrase 'never before'." The article outlined Trump's swift use of executive orders to undo Obama's work for the environment. This, too, was a significant point especially since Trump would soon announce his decision on whether or not to withdraw from the Paris Agreement, which Obama had entered into to push his environmental agenda. In fact, on the 100th day, thousands marched on Washington D.C. to protest Trump's climate change policies. Furthermore, Trump also worked to undo Obama's trade decisions and business regulations. The New York Times also reminded the public of Trump's conflicting business holdings, of his hidden tax returns, and that he had "turned the White House into a family-run enterprise," resembling a reality TV-show with all of its intrigue. That the White House had changed Trump, however, was echoed by the president himself. "I never realized how big it was," Trump stated in an interview. "Every decision is much harder than you'd normally make." Later on, he concluded, "This is more work than in my previous life. I thought it would be easier."[14] On the other side, Senate Minority Leader Chuck Schumer, who was no stranger to the difficulties of Congress, viewed Trump's 100 days as filled with "broken promises to the working people of America," saying "the president's first 100 days have hardly been a success." But despite the difficulty and criticism, Trump felt that he was up to the task and boasted that his first 100 days must have been nearly the most successful in the country's history.[15]

President Trump certainly worked very hard to achieve his goals during the first 100 days. He may have been behind in filling administration posts, but he certainly was ahead in

TWEET THE TRUTH

passing executive orders, even if some had been halted by supreme court judges. He had attempted to replace Obamacare, but had failed to get support from the conservatives in Congress. Nonetheless, a repeal and replacement would surely come. His goal was especially to boost the economy and bring jobs back to America. In this, he had achieved some success. For example, as he reminded listeners at his final rally in Harrisburg, the Dakota Access pipeline brought thousands of jobs to America. He had also influenced major American companies to build new factories in the US. Furthermore, the stock market had shot upward to record highs during the brief time since Trump winning the election and becoming president. Therefore, there was a general attitude of financial stability under the Trump presidency.

During the first 100 days, the media presented the facts as they saw it. For them, it was truth. For the president, it was fake news. Over just a short period of time since Trump became president, "fake news" had become a household word. He often leveled the words at CNN, the New York Times, the Washington Post, and MSNBC. At the same time, he added that he loved the media – just not when it presents fake news. The media often came back with the same "fake" accusation at Trump, accusing him of spouting falsities. How intriguing it was though, that the president often wrote the storyline for the following weeks of news stories with a single tweet.

What would the next 100 days bring? Who could tell. The previous relationship however, predicted a rocky future. Would Trump back off from more conservative stances to

Presidency Under Pressure

please the media and Democrats? Unlikely. Although, the media seemed sure he was far too conservative for them. What was more, he was moving in unpredictable directions which tended to confuse traditional journalism. It had certainly been 100 days of war between Trump and the media, with the latter constantly putting pressure on the presidency. Trump felt attacked at nearly every turn, but the media was left on its guard, wondering what the next pre-dawn presidential tweet would hold in store.

NOTES

CHAPTER I

NOTES

[1] "Election 2016: AP Calls Wisconsin—And Presidency—For Donald Trump," *DCist*, accessed January 21, 2017, http://dcist.com/2016/11/election_2016_results.php; Friendz Fun Club, *US Election Day 2016 Live - Live Result America Election*, 2016, https://www.youtube.com/watch?v=XxTTh9O21HM; "LIVE BLOG: Election Night 2016," *NPR.Org*, accessed January 21, 2017, http://www.npr.org/2016/11/08/500427835/live-blog-election-night-2016.

[2] Friendz Fun Club, *US Election Day 2016 Live - Live Result America Election*.

[3] Marina Fang, "President Obama Tells Working Class Voters Not To Be 'Bamboozled' By Trump," *Huffington Post*, November 1, 2016, sec. Politics, http://www.huffingtonpost.com/entry/obama-trump-working-class_us_5819111ee4b00f11fc5c6fdc; {#pmad-Byline-Frame{width:620px !important; Height:120px !important;}}, "President Obama Tells a Donald Trump Horror Story for Halloween on 'Samantha Bee,'" *Business Insider*, accessed January 21, 2017, http://www.businessinsider.com/barack-obama-full-frontal-samantha-bee-interview-donald-trump-2016-11.

[4] "What Are the Odds of Trump, Clinton Winning the 2016 Presidential Election?," *WREG.Com*, November 1, 2016, http://wreg.com/2016/11/01/what-are-the-odds-of-trump-clinton-winning-the-2016-presidential-election/.

[5] "Hillary Clinton Emails: How FBI Investigation Might Affect the Presidential Race," *Fox8.Com*, October 31, 2016, http://fox8.com/2016/10/31/hillary-clinton-emails-how-fbi-investigation-might-affect-the-presidential-race/.

[6] Larry Celona, Richard Johnson, and Bruce Golding, "Hillary Already Planning Her Giant Victory Celebration," *New York Post*, October 31, 2016, http://nypost.com/2016/10/31/hillary-planning-

NOTES

election-night-fireworks-show-on-hudson-river/.

[7] Kailani KoenigFrank Thorp V, "Ohio Gov. John Kasich, Disliking Trump and Clinton, Votes McCain for President," *NBC News*, accessed March 3, 2017, http://www.nbcnews.com/card/ohio-gov-john-kasich-disliking-trump-clinton-votes-mccain-president-n675996; "In Trump, Italy Sees 'Berlusconi Americano,'" *US News & World Report*, accessed March 3, 2017, https://www.usnews.com/news/best-countries/articles/2016-11-01/italians-see-similarities-between-donald-trump-and-silvio-berlusconi; "Ku Klux Klan Newspaper Supports Donald Trump For President," *Fortune*, accessed March 3, 2017, http://fortune.com/2016/11/02/donald-trump-ku-klux-klan-newspaper/; Kurt Eichenwald On 11/4/16 at 5:50 AM, "Why Russia Is Backing Donald Trump," *Newsweek*, November 4, 2016, http://www.newsweek.com/donald-trump-vladimir-putin-russia-hillary-clinton-united-states-europe-516895; David A. Graham, "Which Republicans Oppose Donald Trump? A Cheat Sheet," *The Atlantic*, November 6, 2016, https://www.theatlantic.com/politics/archive/2016/11/where-republicans-stand-on-donald-trump-a-cheat-sheet/481449/; Cyra Master, "Final newspaper endorsement count: Clinton 57, Trump 2," Text, *TheHill*, (November 6, 2016), http://thehill.com/blogs/ballot-box/presidential-races/304606-final-newspaper-endorsement-count-clinton-57-trump-2.

[8] Michael Calderone, "A Donald Trump Presidency Presents A Grave Threat To The Press," *Huffington Post*, November 7, 2016, sec. Media, http://www.huffingtonpost.com/entry/donald-trump-press-threat_us_5820e469e4b0e80b02cbe800.

[9] Amy Goodman, "Michael Moore: If Elected, Donald Trump Would Be 'Last President of the United States,'" *AlterNet*, November 7, 2016, http://www.alternet.org/election-2016/michael-moore-if-elected-donald-trump-would-be-last-president-united-states.

[10] Dominique Fortes, "Donald Trump's Neighbor: I Would Be 'Scared to Death' of Having Him as Our President," *CNBC*, November 7, 2016, http://www.cnbc.com/2016/11/07/donald-trumps-neighbor-i-would-be-scared-to-death-of-having-him-as-our-president.html.

NOTES

[11] "Why Trump Should Not Be President of the United States," *Rolling Stone*, accessed March 3, 2017, http://www.rollingstone.com/politics/features/donald-trump-cannot-be-president-of-the-united-states-w448907.

[12] José Ramos-Horta, Oscar Arias, and John Hume, "Nobel Peace Laureates Warn: Trump Presidency Would Bring Grave Risks," *Huffington Post*, November 6, 2016, http://www.huffingtonpost.com/jose-ramoshorta/nobel-peace-laureates-war_b_12824666.html.

[13] "Donald Trump Still Has No Business Winning the Presidential Race," *Washington Post*, accessed March 3, 2017, https://www.washingtonpost.com/news/the-fix/wp/2016/11/05/donald-trump-still-has-no-business-winning-the-presidential-race/.

[14] Ibid.; Dana Milbank and Dana Milbank, "The First 100 Horrific Days of a Trump Presidency," *The Washington Post*, November 4, 2016, https://www.washingtonpost.com/opinions/the-first-100-horrific-days-of-a-trump-presidency/2016/11/04/1abca4d2-a286-11e6-a44d-cc2898cfab06_story.html?utm_term=.850ccbdec98c; "Strategies for Surviving a Trump Administration," *Washington Post*, accessed March 3, 2017, https://www.washingtonpost.com/posteverything/wp/2016/11/02/strategies-for-surviving-a-trump-administration/.

[15] Tom Kludt CNN, "New Tracking Poll: Trump, Clinton in Tight Race," *CNN*, accessed March 3, 2017, http://www.cnn.com/2016/11/01/politics/presidential-poll-donald-trump-hillary-clinton-abc/index.html; Maggie Haberman, "Presidential Election: Melania Trump and Bernie Sanders to the Rescue," *The New York Times*, November 3, 2016, https://www.nytimes.com/2016/11/03/us/politics/presidential-election.html.

[16] "How Donald Trump Drove down Presidential Spending," *USA TODAY*, accessed March 3, 2017, http://www.usatoday.com/story/news/politics/elections/2016/2016/11/07/how-donald-trump-drove-down-presidential-spending/93435504/.

Notes

[17] "Column: The Stock Market Doesn't like the Idea of a Trump Presidency," *PBS NewsHour*, accessed March 3, 2017, http://www.pbs.org/newshour/making-sense/column-stock-market-doesnt-like-idea-trump-presidency/.

[18] Kevin Liptak Producer CNN White House, "Michelle Obama: I Went to Bed before Trump Won," *CNN*, accessed December 7, 2016, http://www.cnn.com/2016/12/07/politics/michelle-obama-election-night-people-interview/index.html.

[19] The New York Times, "Donald Trump Completes Final Lap, Electoral College, to White House," *The New York Times*, December 19, 2016, http://www.nytimes.com/2016/12/19/us/politics/electoral-college-vote.html.

[20] https://www.facebook.com/BobWoodward, "President-Elect Donald Trump Is about to Learn the Nation's 'Deep Secrets,'" *Washington Post*, accessed April 26, 2017, https://www.washingtonpost.com/world/national-security/president-elect-donald-trump-is-about-to-learn-the-nations-deep-secrets/2016/11/12/8bf9bc40-a847-11e6-8fc0-7be8f848c492_story.html.

[21] Nolan D. McCaskill, "Obama Reminds Trump: 'There's Only One President at a Time,'" *POLITICO*, accessed April 27, 2017, http://politi.co/2fzO6tI.

Chapter II

[1] "Trump: No 'Big' Vacations, No Salary as President," *USA TODAY*, accessed April 26, 2017, https://www.usatoday.com/story/news/politics/onpolitics/2016/11/13/donald-trump-60-minutes-vacation-salary/93778704/; "Will President-Elect Trump Live in the White House or New York?," *BBC News*, November 14, 2016, sec. US & Canada, http://www.bbc.com/news/world-us-canada-37972044.

[2] Tanzina Vega, "President Trump and Civil Rights: The Biggest Fears," *CNNMoney*, November 11, 2016, http://money.cnn.com/2016/11/11/news/trump-president-civil-rights/index.html; "Losing the Popular Vote Won't Rein in President

NOTES

Trump," *The New Yorker*, November 11, 2016, http://www.newyorker.com/news/news-desk/losing-the-popular-vote-wont-rein-in-president-trump; "Here's What President Donald Trump Plans to Do in His First 100 Days," *Philly.Com*, November 10, 2016, http://www.philly.com/philly/blogs/real-time/Heres-what-President-Donald-Trump-plans-to-do-in-his-first-100-days.html; "What President Trump Means for Your Pocketbook," *USA TODAY*, accessed April 26, 2017, https://www.usatoday.com/story/money/columnist/powell/2016/11/09/what-president-trump-means-your-pocketbook/93522982/.
[3] Pervaiz Shallwani, Kate King, and Trisha Thadani, "Protests Against President-Elect Donald Trump Continue Across the U.S.," *Wall Street Journal*, November 13, 2016, sec. US, http://www.wsj.com/articles/donald-trump-protests-continue-in-u-s-person-injured-in-portland-1478955985.
[4] "Anti-Trump Protests: Portland Police Call It 'Riot' - CNN.Com," accessed November 27, 2016, http://www.cnn.com/2016/11/11/us/oregon-protest-riot/; "'Not My President': Thousands Protest Trump in Rallies across the U.S.," *Washington Post*, accessed November 27, 2016, https://www.washingtonpost.com/news/post-politics/wp/2016/11/10/not-my-president-thousand-protest-trump-in-rallies-across-the-u-s/.
[5] "Obama to Anti-Trump Protesters: March On," Text.Article, *FoxNews.Com*, (November 17, 2016), http://www.foxnews.com/politics/2016/11/17/obama-to-anti-trump-protesters-march-on.html.
[6] "Protests Continue on Fifth Straight Day Denouncing Donald Trump as President," *USA TODAY*, accessed April 27, 2017, https://www.usatoday.com/story/news/2016/11/13/protests-sunday-donald-trump-president/93769564/; Shallwani, King, and Thadani, "Protests Against President-Elect Donald Trump Continue Across the U.S."
[7] "Donald Trump's First, Alarming Week as President-Elect," *The New Yorker*, November 16, 2016, http://www.newyorker.com/news/daily-comment/donald-trumps-first-

NOTES

alarming-week-as-president-elect.

[8] "Vice President-Elect Mike Pence Set To Govern At Trump's Side," *NPR.Org*, accessed April 27, 2017, http://www.npr.org/2016/11/16/502214241/vice-president-elect-mike-pence-set-to-govern-at-trumps-side.

[9] A. B. C. News, "How the World's Strongman Leaders See a Trump Presidency," *ABC News*, November 16, 2016, http://abcnews.go.com/International/strongman-leaders-world-react-president-elected-trump/story?id=43577046; Daniel Halper, "Trump to Meet with First Foreign Leader as President-Elect," *New York Post*, November 17, 2016, http://nypost.com/2016/11/17/trump-to-meet-with-first-foreign-leader-as-president-elect/.

[10] "FBI and CIA Give Differing Accounts to Lawmakers on Russia's Motives in 2016 Hacks," *Washington Post*, accessed December 12, 2016, https://www.washingtonpost.com/world/national-security/fbi-and-cia-give-differing-accounts-to-lawmakers-on-russias-motives-in-2016-hacks/2016/12/10/c6dfadfa-bef0-11e6-94ac-3d324840106c_story.html.

[11] "Trump Dismisses CIA Findings of Russian Election Tampering," *USA TODAY*, accessed December 12, 2016, http://www.usatoday.com/story/news/politics/2016/12/11/trump-dismisses-allegations-russian-election-tampering/95297756/.

[12] A. B. C. News, "Trump Engages CIA in War of Words Over Russian Election Hacking," *ABC News*, December 12, 2016, http://abcnews.go.com/International/trump-war-words-intelligence-officials-amid-disagreement-russian/story?id=44131322.

[13] "Trump Taps Loyalists for Cabinet Picks: Session for AG, Pompeo as CIA Director," Text.Article, *FoxNews.Com*, (November 18, 2016), http://www.foxnews.com/politics/2016/11/18/alabama-senator-sessions-offered-attorney-general-post-in-trump-administration.html.

[14] "South Carolina Gov. Nikki Haley Named As Trump's Ambassador To The U.N. : NPR," accessed May 15, 2017, http://www.npr.org/2016/11/23/503182752/south-carolina-gov-nikki-haley-named-as-trumps-ambassador-to-the-u-n.

NOTES

[15] "Trump Chooses South Carolina Gov. Nikki Haley as UN Ambassador | Fox News," accessed November 27, 2016, http://www.foxnews.com/politics/2016/11/23/trump-chooses-south-carolina-gov-nikki-haley-as-un-ambassador.html; Eugene Scott CNN Jim Acosta and Sara Murray, "Trump Picks Haley to Be US Ambassador to UN," *CNN*, accessed November 27, 2016, http://www.cnn.com/2016/11/23/politics/nikki-haley-picked-for-un-ambassador/index.html.

[16] Mark Landler and Maggie Haberman, "Trump Diversifies Cabinet; Picks Nikki Haley and Betsy DeVos," *The New York Times*, November 23, 2016, http://www.nytimes.com/2016/11/23/us/politics/donald-trump-president-elect.html.

[17] Mahita Gajanan, "Donald Trump Outlines Policy Plans for First 100 Days in Office," *Time*, accessed April 27, 2017, http://time.com/4579404/donald-trump-policy-video/; James Masters CNN, "Trump's First 100 Days: A Breakdown of His Plan," *CNN*, accessed April 27, 2017, http://www.cnn.com/2016/11/22/politics/trump-first-100-days-plan/index.html; "Here's How Trump's Plan to Defund Sanctuary Cities Could Play out," *NY Daily News*, accessed April 27, 2017, http://www.nydailynews.com/news/politics/trump-plan-defund-sanctuary-cities-play-article-1.2885423.

[18] "President-Elect Trump Can't Be in the Trump Business," *Los Angeles Times*, November 15, 2016, http://www.latimes.com/opinion/editorials/la-ed-trump-conflicts-of-interest-20161114-story.html; "How President Trump Could Use the White House to Enrich Himself and His Family," *Washington Post*, accessed April 27, 2017, https://www.washingtonpost.com/posteverything/wp/2016/11/18/how-president-trump-could-use-the-white-house-to-enrich-himself-and-his-family/.

[19] Chuck Todd, Mark Murray, and Carrie Dann, "How Trump's Business Presents Huge Conflicts of Interest," *NBC News*, November 21, 2016, http://www.nbcnews.com/politics/first-read/how-trump-s-business-presents-huge-conflicts-interest-n686651.

NOTES

[20] Ian Swanson, "Questions swirl around Trump business announcement," Text, *TheHill*, (November 30, 2016), http://thehill.com/homenews/administration/308167-questions-swirl-around-trump-business-announcement.

[21] Jill Disis, "Donald Trump Says He's Turning Away 'Billions' but Has 'the Right' to Do Business Deals," *CNNMoney*, December 11, 2016, http://money.cnn.com/2016/12/11/news/companies/donald-trump-business-conflicts/index.html.

[22] "Trump Says His Two Oldest Sons, Other Executives Will Handle His Businesses during Presidency," Text.Article, *FoxNews.Com*, (December 13, 2016), http://www.foxnews.com/politics/2016/12/13/trump-says-his-two-oldest-sons-other-executives-will-handle-his-businesses-during-presidency.html.

[23] "Trump Plans To Dissolve His Foundation; N.Y. Attorney General Pushes Back," *NPR.Org*, accessed December 28, 2016, http://www.npr.org/sections/thetwo-way/2016/12/24/506852411/trump-plans-to-dissolve-his-foundation-n-y-attorney-general-pushes-back.

[24] Laura Jarrett CNN, "Judge Orders Trump Sit for 7-Hour Deposition in Early January," *CNN*, accessed December 16, 2016, http://www.cnn.com/2016/12/14/politics/donald-trump-deposition-washington-hotel/index.html.

[25] "The Reality Show President: Trump to Retain Producing Credit on 'Celebrity Apprentice,'" *Washington Post*, accessed December 9, 2016, https://www.washingtonpost.com/politics/the-reality-show-president-trump-to-retain-producing-credit-on-celebrity-apprentice/2016/12/08/0e7eada2-bd9b-11e6-ac85-094a21c44abc_story.html.

[26] "Donald Trump Denies He Will Work on The Apprentice While President," *BBC News*, December 10, 2016, sec. Entertainment & Arts, http://www.bbc.com/news/entertainment-arts-38275732.

[27] "The Reality Show President."

[28] "Preparing for White House, Trump to Attend Army-Navy Game," Text.Article, *FoxSports*, (December 10, 2016), http://www.foxnews.com/sports/2016/12/10/preparing-for-white-

NOTES

house-trump-to-attend-army-navy-game.html.
[29] David Wright CNN, "Trump Aide: No Plan to Pursue Charges against Clinton," *CNN*, accessed November 22, 2016, http://www.cnn.com/2016/11/22/politics/conway-no-clinton-charges-donald-trump/index.html.
[30] "Trump Cancels Meeting with 'Failing' New York Times -- Then Reverses Course," Text.Article, *FoxNews.Com*, (November 22, 2016), http://www.foxnews.com/politics/2016/11/22/trump-cancels-meeting-with-failing-new-york-times-then-reverses-course.html.

CHAPTER III

[1] Eun Kyung Kim, "TIME Person of the Year for 2016 Is President-Elect Donald Trump," *TODAY.Com*, December 7, 2016, http://www.today.com/news/president-elect-donald-trump-time-person-year-2016-t105684.
[2] Andrew O'Reilly, "Europe's Trump Moment: Countries See Rise of Populist Leaders amid Anger over Economy, Migrant Crisis," Text.Article, *FoxNews.Com*, (November 30, 2016), http://www.foxnews.com/world/2016/11/30/europes-trump-moment-countries-see-rise-populist-leaders-amid-anger-over-economy-migrant-crisis.html; "Alec Baldwin Says He'll Stop Trump Impersonation If the President-Elect Releases His Tax Records," *PEOPLE.Com*, December 4, 2016, http://people.com/politics/alec-baldwin-stop-donald-trump-impersonation-tax-records-snl/.
[3] Riva Gold and Ira Iosebashvili, "U.S. Stocks Climb, Extending Rally," *Wall Street Journal*, December 8, 2016, sec. Markets, http://www.wsj.com/articles/stocks-advance-after-wall-street-highs-1481186556.
[4] "Trump Momentum Powers Wall Street to Fresh Records, Dow Closes Above 19K | Fox Business," accessed November 27, 2016, http://www.foxbusiness.com/markets/2016/11/22/trump-momentum-powers-wall-street-to-fresh-records.html.
[5] "After Carrier Deal, Trump Vows Tax of 35 Percent for US Business Going Overseas," Text.Article, *FoxNews.Com*, (December 4, 2016), http://www.foxnews.com/politics/2016/12/04/after-carrier-

NOTES

deal-trump-vows-tax-35-percent-for-us-business-going-overseas.html; Nelson D. Schwartz, "Vowing to Squeeze Businesses, Trump Has Tactics Challenged," *The New York Times*, December 4, 2016, http://www.nytimes.com/2016/12/04/us/politics/trump-takes-twitter-aim-at-companies-looking-to-move-jobs-abroad.html.

[6] John Schwartz Lipton Jennifer Steinhauer, Eric and Ron Nixon, "Trump Meets With Al Gore on Climate Change While House G.O.P. Rebuffs Tariff Plan," *The New York Times*, December 5, 2016, http://www.nytimes.com/2016/12/05/us/politics/donald-trump-transition.html.

[7] Suzanne O'Halloran, "Trump Strikes Deal With Carrier, Ford, What About Oreo?," Text.Article, *FOXBusiness*, (November 30, 2016), http://www.foxbusiness.com/politics/2016/11/30/trump-strikes-deal-with-carrier-ford-what-about-oreo.html.

[8] The Associated Press, "Scuttled Ford Plant Has Mexico Fearing More Under Trump," *The New York Times*, January 4, 2017, http://www.nytimes.com/aponline/2017/01/04/world/americas/ap-lt-mexico-ford.html.

[9] Arthur Delaney and Daniel Marans, "Bernie Sanders: Donald Trump 'Has Endangered' U.S. Jobs With Carrier Deal," *Huffington Post*, December 1, 2016, sec. Politics, http://www.huffingtonpost.com/entry/bernie-sanders-donald-trump-has-endangered-american-jobs_us_58402e52e4b09e21702cdedc.

[10] Jackie Calmes Martin Jonathan and Jennifer Steinhauer, "Donald Trump in Indiana as Democratic Ranks Crack. Chris Christie for G.O.P. Chairman?," *The New York Times*, December 1, 2016, http://www.nytimes.com/2016/12/01/us/politics/donald-trump-transition.html.

[11] "After Carrier Deal, Trump Vows Tax of 35 Percent for US Business Going Overseas."

[12] Schwartz, "Vowing to Squeeze Businesses, Trump Has Tactics Challenged."

[13] "Trump Nominees Map out Plans for Tax Cuts, Trade and Carrier-Style Negotiations," *Washington Post*, accessed December 1, 2016, https://www.washingtonpost.com/business/economy/trump-nominees-map-out-plans-for-tax-cuts-trade-and-carrier-style-

NOTES

negotiations/2016/11/30/54cfca98-b73d-11e6-a677-b608fbb3aaf6_story.html; "Pence Makes Indiana Taxpayers Part of Trump Carrier Jobs Plan," *MSNBC*, November 30, 2016, http://www.msnbc.com/rachel-maddow/watch/pence-makes-indiana-taxpayers-part-of-trump-carrier-jobs-plan-821559363758.

[14] "Donald Trump Insulted a Union Leader on Twitter. Then the Phone Started to Ring.," *Washington Post*, accessed December 9, 2016, https://www.washingtonpost.com/news/wonk/wp/2016/12/07/donald-trump-retaliated-against-a-union-leader-on-twitter-then-his-phone-started-to-ring/.

[15] "8,000 U.S. Jobs? Trump Takes Credit for Sprint, Start-up Decisions," accessed January 4, 2017, http://www.usatoday.com/story/tech/2016/12/28/trump-sprint-moving-5000-jobs-back-us-oneweb-add-3000-more/95932894/.

[16] Associated Press, "Crowd Shouts 'No Romney!' At Trump 'Thank You' Rally," *New York Post*, December 5, 2016, http://nypost.com/2016/12/04/crowd-shouts-no-romney-at-trump-thank-you-rally/.

[17] "In Trump's GOP, Jeff Sessions Goes from Fringe to Prime Time," *Washington Post*, accessed December 1, 2016, https://www.washingtonpost.com/politics/in-trumps-gop-sessions-rockets-from-the-fringe-to-prime-time/2016/07/18/1fc04d14-490b-11e6-acbc-4d4870a079da_story.html.

[18] Andrew Rafferty, "Donald Trump's Cabinet Picks so Far," *NBC News*, November 30, 2016, http://www.nbcnews.com/politics/politics-news/donald-trump-s-cabinet-picks-so-far-n690296.

[19] CNBC, "In Trump Cabinet, Commerce Secretary Pick Wilbur Ross Will Run Trade Policy," *CNBC*, December 21, 2016, http://www.cnbc.com/2016/12/21/in-trump-cabinet-commerce-secretary-will-run-trade-policy.html.

[20] Landon Thomas Jr and Alexandra Stevenson, "Trump's Economic Cabinet Picks Signal Embrace of Wall St. Elite," *The New York Times*, November 30, 2016, http://www.nytimes.com/2016/11/30/business/dealbook/trumps-

NOTES

economic-cabinet-picks-signal-embrace-of-wall-st-elite.html; "Trump Nominees Map out Plans for Tax Cuts, Trade and Carrier-Style Negotiations."

[21] Jacob Pramuk, "Trump Just Offered yet Another Goldman Veteran a Spot in His Administration," *CNBC*, December 9, 2016, http://www.cnbc.com/2016/12/09/trump-offers-goldman-sachs-president-gary-cohn-directorship-of-national-economic-council-nbc-news.html.

[22] "Mad Dog, as in 'Mad Dog' Mattis: The Colorful History of a Great American Nickname," *Washington Post*, accessed December 2, 2016, https://www.washingtonpost.com/news/morning-mix/wp/2016/12/02/trumps-pick-for-secretary-of-defense-is-known-as-mad-dog-heres-the-history-of-the-nickname/; "First Read's Morning Clips: Mad Dog," *NBC News*, December 2, 2016, http://www.nbcnews.com/politics/first-read/first-read-s-morning-clips-mad-dog-n691091.

[23] "Mattis Says He's 'Grateful' to Be Nominated as Defense Secretary; House GOP Introduces Waiver Language," Text.Article, *FoxNews.Com*, (December 6, 2016), http://www.foxnews.com/politics/2016/12/06/mattis-says-hes-grateful-to-be-nominated-as-defense-secretary-house-gop-introduces-waiver-language.html.

[24] Mark Landler and Maggie Haberman, "Donald Trump Picks John Kelly, Retired General, to Lead Homeland Security," *The New York Times*, December 7, 2016, http://www.nytimes.com/2016/12/07/us/politics/john-kelly-dhs-trump.html.

[25] Christopher Lamb, "President-Elect Trump Calls for Removal of Statue of Liberty Because It Encourages Immigration," *Huffington Post*, November 18, 2016, http://www.huffingtonpost.com/christopher-lamb/presidentelect-trump-call_b_13077746.html.

[26] "Trump Nominated Carson to Lead U.S. Housing, Urban Policy," *Washington Post*, accessed December 5, 2016, https://www.washingtonpost.com/news/powerpost/wp/2016/12/05/trump-to-nominate-carson-to-lead-u-s-housing-urban-policy/.

NOTES

[27] "Trump Names Scott Pruitt, Oklahoma Attorney General Suing EPA on Climate Change, to Head the EPA," *Washington Post*, accessed December 9, 2016, https://www.washingtonpost.com/news/energy-environment/wp/2016/12/07/trump-names-scott-pruitt-oklahoma-attorney-general-suing-epa-on-climate-change-to-head-the-epa/.

[28] Amy Harder and Michael C. Bender, "Trump Expected to Pick Rep. Cathy McMorris Rodgers to Run Interior," *Wall Street Journal*, December 9, 2016, sec. Politics, http://www.wsj.com/articles/trump-expected-to-pick-rep-cathy-mcmorris-rodgers-to-run-interior-1481298518.

[29] Nick Timiraos and Andrew Tangel, "Donald Trump's Cabinet Selections Signal Deregulation Moves Are Coming," *Wall Street Journal*, December 9, 2016, sec. Politics, http://www.wsj.com/articles/donald-trump-cabinet-picks-signal-deregulation-moves-are-coming-1481243006.

[30] Jim Acosta CNN Eugene Scott and John King, "Tillerson Leading Candidate for Secretary of State," *CNN*, accessed December 12, 2016, http://www.cnn.com/2016/12/10/politics/rex-tillerson-secretary-of-state/index.html.

[31] "'Embodiment of the American Dream' Is Trump's Secretary of State Pick," *NBC News*, December 13, 2016, http://www.nbcnews.com/politics/politics-news/trump-names-rex-tillerson-nominee-secretary-state-n695281; "Kissinger, a Longtime Putin Confidant, Sidles up to Trump," *POLITICO*, accessed December 24, 2016, http://politi.co/2i2xrkl.

[32] "Trump Winning GOP Converts with Cabinet Picks - POLITICO," accessed December 12, 2016, http://www.politico.com/story/2016/12/trump-cabinet-picks-gop-converts-232450.

[33] Nicholas Fandos, "Trump Still Hasn't Named a Democrat to His Cabinet," *The New York Times*, December 16, 2016, http://www.nytimes.com/2016/12/16/us/politics/donald-trump-appointments-democrats.html.

NOTES

[34] "Trump Unwinds Some Foreign Deals but Many Potential Conflicts Remain," *Los Angeles Times*, accessed December 22, 2016, http://www.latimes.com/nation/politics/trailguide/la-na-trailguide-updates-trump-stops-the-drain-the-swamp-talk-as-1482346628-htmlstory.html.

[35] "Donald Trump Taps Rick Perry To Head Agency He Once Forgot," *NPR.Org*, accessed December 14, 2016, http://www.npr.org/2016/12/13/505397228/donald-trump-taps-rick-perry-to-head-agency-he-once-forgot.

[36] "Former Georgia Governor Said to Be Trump's Pick for Agriculture Secretary - Chicago Tribune," accessed January 5, 2017, http://www.chicagotribune.com/news/nationworld/politics/ct-donald-trump-sonny-perdue-agriculture-secretary-20170102-story.html; "Trump Meets With Candidates for Agriculture Secretary - ABC News," accessed January 4, 2017, http://abcnews.go.com/Politics/wireStory/trump-meets-candidates-agriculture-secretary-44476270.

[37] "Trump Recruits Controversial Advisers to Help Shape Administration's Trade, Regulatory Strategy," *Washington Post*, accessed December 22, 2016, https://www.washingtonpost.com/news/wonk/wp/2016/12/21/trump-appointments-signal-he-might-stick-with-hard-line-stances-on-trade-regulations/.

[38] "Trump Unwinds Some Foreign Deals but Many Potential Conflicts Remain."

CHAPTER IV

[1] Eugene Scott CNN, "Donald Trump: Fidel Castro Is Dead!," *CNN*, accessed November 27, 2016, http://www.cnn.com/2016/11/26/politics/trump-reacts-to-castro-death/index.html; "Obama: History Will Judge Fidel Castro's 'Enormous Impact' on Cubans," *Washington Post*, accessed November 27, 2016, https://www.washingtonpost.com/news/the-fix/wp/2016/11/26/obama-history-will-judge-fidel-castros-enormous-impact-on-cubans/.

Notes

[2] O'Reilly, "Europe's Trump Moment."
[3] Karl Vick, "What Donald Trump's Pick for Ambassador to Israel Means," *Time*, December 16, 2016, http://time.com/4605223/donald-trump-israel-david-friedman/.
[4] Nahal Toosi, "Trump Calls on Obama to Veto U.N. Resolution on Israeli Settlements," *POLITICO*, accessed December 22, 2016, http://politi.co/2hg8ODx.
[5] "China Treads Carefully as Trump's Taiwan Call Gives Jolt to Ties," *Bloomberg.Com/Politics*, December 3, 2016, http://www.bloomberg.com/politics/articles/2016-12-03/china-dismisses-unprecedented-trump-tsai-call-as-taiwan-gimmick; "Unprecedented Trump-Taiwan Call Was No Surprise — Official," *NBC News*, December 3, 2016, http://www.nbcnews.com/news/world/donald-trump-s-call-taiwan-president-was-not-surprised-official-n691466.
[6] Joseph Weber, "Conway: Trump's Talk with Taiwan Leader 'Just a Call,' Not a Sign of Policy Shift," Text.Article, *FoxNews.Com*, (December 4, 2016), http://www.foxnews.com/politics/2016/12/04/conway-trumps-talk-with-taiwan-leader-just-call-not-sign-policy-shift.html.
[7] "Trump Renews China Criticism, Visits Ohio State Attack Victims on 'Thank You' Tour," Text.Article, *FoxNews.Com*, (December 8, 2016), http://www.foxnews.com/politics/2016/12/08/trump-renews-china-criticism-visits-ohio-state-attack-victims-on-thank-tour.html.
[8] Chris Isidore Marsh Jon Ostrower and Rene, "Trump Wants to Cancel Air Force One Order from Boeing," *CNNMoney*, December 6, 2016, http://money.cnn.com/2016/12/06/news/companies/trump-air-force-one-boeing/index.html.
[9] Paul R. La Monica, "Donald Trump Attacks F-35 Maker for 'out of Control' Costs," *CNNMoney*, December 12, 2016, http://money.cnn.com/2016/12/12/investing/donald-trump-lockheed-martin-f-35-tweet/index.html.
[10] "Trump Recruits Controversial Advisers to Help Shape Administration's Trade, Regulatory Strategy."

Notes

[11] "UPDATE 1-Lockheed Shares Sink Further on Trump's F-35 Threat - Business Insider," accessed December 24, 2016, http://www.businessinsider.com/r-update-1-lockheed-shares-sink-further-on-trumps-f-35-threat-2016-12.

[12] Lipton and Nixon, "Trump Meets With Al Gore on Climate Change While House G.O.P. Rebuffs Tariff Plan."

[13] "Trump Says 'Nobody Really Knows' If Climate Change Is Real," *Washington Post*, accessed December 14, 2016, https://www.washingtonpost.com/news/energy-environment/wp/2016/12/11/trump-says-nobody-really-knows-if-climate-change-is-real/.

[14] Devin Henry, "Dems push for investigation into Trump team's Energy letter," Text, *TheHill*, (December 16, 2016), http://thehill.com/policy/energy-environment/310808-dems-push-for-investigation-into-trump-teams-energy-letter.

[15] A. B. C. News, "Mike Flynn Jr. Forced Out of Trump Transition Amid Fake News Controversy," *ABC News*, December 6, 2016, http://abcnews.go.com/Politics/mike-flynn-jr-forced-trump-transition-amid-fake/story?id=44018995.

[16] A. B. C. News, "Clinton Decries Rise of Fake News in Capitol Speech," *ABC News*, December 9, 2016, http://abcnews.go.com/Politics/wireStory/clinton-decries-rise-fake-news-speech-loss-44080320.

[17] "Clinton Campaign Will Participate in Wisconsin Recount, with an Eye on 'Outside Interference,' Lawyer Says," *Washington Post*, accessed November 27, 2016, https://www.washingtonpost.com/news/post-nation/wp/2016/11/26/clinton-campaign-will-participate-in-wisconsin-recount-with-an-eye-on-outside-interference-lawyer-says/.

[18] "Jill Stein -- Fighting Election Fraud or Lining Her Own Pockets?," Text.Article, *FoxNews.Com*, (November 28, 2016), http://www.foxnews.com/politics/2016/11/28/jill-stein-fighting-election-fraud-or-lining-her-own-pockets.html.

[19] Phil McCausl, "With No Evidence, Trump Makes 'Reckless' Claim 'Millions' Voted Illegally," *NBC News*, November 28, 2016, http://www.nbcnews.com/politics/2016-election/tweet-flurry-

NOTES

president-elect-donald-trump-calls-recount-efforts-sad-n688761.
[20] "Trump Backers Go to Court to Block Vote Recounts in 3 States - The New York Times," accessed December 3, 2016, http://www.nytimes.com/2016/12/02/us/trump-recounts-wisconsin-michigan-pennsylvania.html?_r=0; "Trump Lawyers Push Back against Mich. Recount, Blast Stein," Text.Article, *FoxNews.Com*, (December 2, 2016), http://www.foxnews.com/politics/2016/12/02/trump-lawyers-push-back-against-mich-recount-blast-stein.html.
[21] A. B. C. News, "Focus of Recount Effort Shifts to Michigan, Pennsylvania," *ABC News*, December 5, 2016, http://abcnews.go.com/Politics/wireStory/michigan-begin-recount-legal-fight-moves-pennsylvania-43976726; "Presidential Recount Begins in 2 Michigan Counties," *USA TODAY*, accessed December 5, 2016, http://www.usatoday.com/story/news/politics/elections/2016/12/05/michigan-presidential-ballots-recount/94983372/.
[22] Paulina Firozi, "Federal judge kills recount effort in Michigan," Text, *TheHill*, (December 7, 2016), http://thehill.com/homenews/campaign/309358-federal-judge-kills-recount-effort-in-michigan.
[23] "Wisconsin Judge Rejects Bid to Stop Election Recount," *Reuters*, December 10, 2016, http://www.reuters.com/article/us-usa-trump-recount-idUSKBN13Y22B.
[24] A. B. C. News, "Recount Efforts End: Trump Wins in Wisconsin, Pennsylvania," *ABC News*, December 12, 2016, http://abcnews.go.com/Politics/wireStory/judges-decision-expected-pennsylvania-recount-case-44139924.
[25] "Time for a Change?," *US News & World Report*, accessed December 14, 2016, http://www.usnews.com/news/the-report/articles/2016-12-13/advocates-call-for-an-end-to-the-electoral-college-after-trumps-win.
[26] Steven Levitsky and Daniel Ziblatt, "Is Donald Trump a Threat to Democracy?," *The New York Times*, December 16, 2016, http://www.nytimes.com/2016/12/16/opinion/sunday/is-donald-trump-a-threat-to-democracy.html.

NOTES

[27] "Senators Push for Select Committee to Investigate Russian Attempts to Interfere with the 2016 Race," *Los Angeles Times*, accessed December 18, 2016, http://www.latimes.com/nation/politics/trailguide/la-na-trailguide-updates-trump-s-electoral-college-win-all-but-1481829256-htmlstory.html.

[28] "Trump Is Stoking His Base on His Pre-Inaugural Tour. But Is He Building Bridges? - The Washington Post," accessed December 18, 2016, https://www.washingtonpost.com/politics/trump-is-stoking-his-base-on-his-pre-inaugural-tour-but-is-he-building-bridges/2016/12/17/a74a0f0a-c3ad-11e6-8422-eac61c0ef74d_story.html?utm_term=.205fbec626ed.

CHAPTER V

[1] "9/11 Record of Republican 'Faithless Elector' Called into Question | Fox News," accessed December 18, 2016, http://www.foxnews.com/politics/2016/12/16/911-record-republican-faithless-elector-called-into-question.html.

[2] "Pro-Donald Trump Electoral College Voters Receive Death Threats - CNN Video," accessed May 15, 2017, http://www.cnn.com/videos/politics/2016/12/16/electors-receive-death-threats-flores-dnt-erin.cnn.

[3] "In Last-Shot Bid, Thousands Urge Electoral College to Block Trump at Monday Vote - The Washington Post," accessed December 18, 2016, https://www.washingtonpost.com/politics/in-last-shot-bid-thousands-urge-electoral-college-to-block-trump-at-monday-vote/2016/12/17/125fa84a-c327-11e6-8422-eac61c0ef74d_story.html?utm_term=.d80387d2c1ad.

[4] "U.S. Officials Say Putin Helped Direct the Use of Hacked Materials," accessed December 16, 2016, http://www.nbcnews.com/news/us-news/u-s-officials-putin-personally-involved-u-s-election-hack-n696146; Christina Wilkie, "Trump Takes A New Tack On Russia Election Scandal," *Huffington Post*, December 16, 2016, sec. Politics, http://www.huffingtonpost.com/entry/donald-trump-russian-

NOTES

espionage-was-a-good-thing-for-america_us_5853ffaee4b0b3ddfd8c272f.

[5] "Debate over Russian Hacking Heats up; Obama Promises Retaliation," *Los Angeles Times*, accessed December 18, 2016, http://www.latimes.com/nation/politics/trailguide/la-na-trailguide-updates-trump-s-electoral-college-win-all-but-1481829256-htmlstory.html.

[6] Edward-Isaac Dovere, "Obama: Trump's Victory Threatens America's Core," *POLITICO*, accessed December 18, 2016, http://politi.co/2hafyPb.

[7] "Russia Election Hack Update: Collusion Alleged Between Trump, Russians, Clinton Campaign Chief Podesta Says [VIDEO]," accessed December 19, 2016, http://www.ibtimes.com/russia-election-hack-update-collusion-alleged-between-trump-russians-clinton-campaign-2462256.

[8] Damian Paletta and Kate O'Keeffe, "Donald Trump's Team Tones Down Skepticism on Russia Hacking Evidence," *Wall Street Journal*, December 19, 2016, sec. Politics, http://www.wsj.com/articles/priebus-says-donald-trump-wants-fbi-view-on-russia-hacking-accusations-1482084741.

[9] "Trump Almost Certain to Win Electoral College Vote, but Nothing's Sure in 2016 Elections," Text.Article, *FoxNews.Com*, (December 18, 2016), 201, http://www.foxnews.com/politics/2016/12/18/trump-almost-certain-to-win-electoral-college-vote-but-nothings-sure-in-2016-elections.html.

[10] "Trump Wins Electoral College Vote; a Few Electors Break Ranks," *Reuters*, December 20, 2016, http://www.reuters.com/article/us-usa-election-electoralcollege-idUSKBN1480FQ; The New York Times, "Donald Trump Completes Final Lap, Electoral College, to White House."

[11] "'Next Idea?' After Electoral College Fail, Anti-Trump Forces Look for New Cause | Fox News," accessed December 21, 2016, http://www.foxnews.com/politics/2016/12/20/next-idea-after-electoral-college-fail-anti-trump-forces-look-for-new-cause.html.

NOTES

[12] "'Rogue One': Exactly the 'Star Wars' Movie We Need as the Age of Trump Dawns - Salon.Com," accessed December 24, 2016, http://www.salon.com/2016/12/24/rogue-one-exactly-the-star-wars-movie-we-need-as-the-age-of-trump-dawns/.

[13] "Obama Grants 78 Pre-Christmas Pardons in Last-Minute Clemency Push," *USA TODAY*, accessed December 21, 2016, http://www.usatoday.com/story/news/politics/2016/12/19/obama-grants-78-pre-christmas-pardons/95615810/; "Obama Set a Record for Commuting Sentences — but He's Not the Most Forgiving President in History," *Public Radio International*, accessed January 19, 2017, https://www.pri.org/stories/2017-01-18/obama-set-record-commuting-sentences-hes-not-most-forgiving-president-history; Charlie Savage, "Chelsea Manning to Be Released Early as Obama Commutes Sentence," *The New York Times*, January 17, 2017, https://www.nytimes.com/2017/01/17/us/politics/obama-commutes-bulk-of-chelsea-mannings-sentence.html.

[14] "President Obama Bans Oil Drilling in Large Areas of Atlantic and Arctic Oceans," *Washington Post*, accessed December 21, 2016, https://www.washingtonpost.com/news/energy-environment/wp/2016/12/20/president-obama-expected-to-ban-oil-drilling-in-large-areas-of-atlantic-and-arctic-oceans/.

[15] "The Electoral College Is Thwarting Our Ability to Battle Global Warming," *Washington Post*, accessed December 21, 2016, https://www.washingtonpost.com/news/energy-environment/wp/2016/12/19/the-electoral-college-is-thwarting-our-ability-to-battle-global-warming/.

[16] Sarah Wheaton, "Liberals Yearning for Obama to Keep up Trump Battle," *POLITICO*, accessed December 21, 2016, http://politi.co/2hEH9Ll.

[17] Kenneth P. Vogel, "Trump Private Security Force 'Playing with Fire,'" *POLITICO*, accessed December 21, 2016, http://politi.co/2hgAMux.

[18] "Donald Trump: US Must Greatly Expand Nuclear Weapons," *BBC News*, December 22, 2016, sec. US & Canada, http://www.bbc.com/news/world-us-canada-38410027.

NOTES

[19] "Donald Trump's Forays Into Foreign Policy Strain Transition - WSJ," accessed December 24, 2016, http://www.wsj.com/articles/let-it-be-an-arms-race-trump-says-1482507844.
[20] "Donald Trump Says U.N. Just a Club for People to 'Have a Good Time' - NBC News," accessed December 28, 2016, http://www.nbcnews.com/news/us-news/donald-trump-says-un-just-club-people-have-good-time-n700386; "Trump Accuses Obama of Putting up 'Roadblocks' to a Smooth Transition," *Washington Post*, accessed December 28, 2016, https://www.washingtonpost.com/news/post-politics/wp/2016/12/28/trump-accuses-obama-of-putting-up-roadblocks-to-a-smooth-transition/.
[21] "Spree of Obama Actions Revives GOP Concerns over 'Midnight' Regs, Agenda | Fox News," accessed December 28, 2016, http://www.foxnews.com/politics/2016/12/26/spree-obama-actions-revives-gop-concerns-over-midnight-regs-agenda.html.
[22] "President Obama Says He Could Have Beaten Trump — Trump Says 'NO WAY!' - The Washington Post," accessed December 28, 2016, https://www.washingtonpost.com/news/post-politics/wp/2016/12/26/president-obama-says-he-would-have-beaten-trump-if-i-had-run-again/?utm_term=.ed15966d9996.
[23] Ashley Alman, "Barack Obama's Pearl Harbor Speech Seen As Rebuke Of Trump World View," *Huffington Post*, December 28, 2016, sec. Politics, http://www.huffingtonpost.com/entry/barack-obama-pearl-harbor_us_5863ccc2e4b0d9a59459a097.
[24] Coral Davenport, "Obama Designates Two New National Monuments, Protecting 1.65 Million Acres," *The New York Times*, December 28, 2016, http://www.nytimes.com/2016/12/28/us/politics/obama-national-monument-bears-ears-utah-gold-butte.html.
[25] Reuters, "U.S. To Transfer 4 Guantanamo Bay Detainees To Saudi Arabia," *Huffington Post*, January 5, 2017, sec. WorldPost, http://www.huffingtonpost.com/entry/guantanamo-detainees-transfer-saudi-arabia_us_586df3b1e4b0c56eb4b71afb.

Notes

[26] "New Party of No? Dems Prepare for Battle with Trump on Cabinet Picks, Agenda | Fox News," accessed December 28, 2016, http://www.foxnews.com/politics/2016/12/27/new-party-no-dems-prepare-for-battle-with-trump-on-cabinet-picks-agenda.html.
[27] "GOP Airs Obamacare Divisions in Pence Meeting," *POLITICO*, accessed January 5, 2017, http://politi.co/2j6miOD.
[28] Leslie Picker, "Donald Trump Nominates Wall Street Lawyer to Head S.E.C.," *The New York Times*, January 4, 2017, http://www.nytimes.com/2017/01/04/business/dealbook/donald-trump-sec-jay-clayton.html.
[29] "Obama Sanctions Russian Officials over Election Hacking," *USA TODAY*, accessed January 5, 2017, http://www.usatoday.com/story/news/politics/2016/12/29/barack-obama-russia-sanctions-vladimir-putin/95958472/.
[30] "Trump Praises Putin over Response to US Sanctions, Calls Him 'Very Smart' | Fox News," accessed January 4, 2017, http://www.foxnews.com/politics/2016/12/30/trump-praises-putin-over-response-to-us-sanctions-calls-him-very-smart.html; "Putin: Russia Won't Expel US Diplomats - CNN.Com," accessed January 4, 2017, http://www.cnn.com/2016/12/30/europe/russia-us-diplomats-expulsion/; "Spicer Hints Obama's Russian Sanctions 'Politically Motivated' | Fox News," accessed January 4, 2017, http://www.foxnews.com/politics/2017/01/02/spicer-hints-obamas-russian-sanctions-politically-motivated.html.
[31] "Donald Trump Ends The Year Again Disputing U.S. Intelligence On Russian Hacking | The Huffington Post," accessed January 4, 2017, http://www.huffingtonpost.com/entry/trump-russian-hacking_us_58686f8de4b0d9a5945bc5e9.
[32] "Trump Sets Long-Awaited News Conference for January 11 | Fox News," accessed January 4, 2017, http://www.foxnews.com/politics/2017/01/03/trump-sets-long-awaited-news-conference-for-january-11.html.
[33] Euan McKirdy CNN, "WikiLeaks' Assange: Russia Didn't Give Us Emails," *CNN*, accessed January 5, 2017, http://www.cnn.com/2017/01/04/politics/assange-wikileaks-hannity-intv/index.html; Jeremy Diamond CNN Evan Perez, Pamela Brown

NOTES

and Jim Sciutto, "Trump Derides Intel Briefing on 'so-Called' Russian Hacking," *CNN*, accessed January 5, 2017, http://www.cnn.com/2017/01/03/politics/donald-trump-intelligence-briefing-russian-hack-delay/index.html; "Intel Report on Russian Interference Finds No Documents Forged," Text.Article, *FoxNews.Com*, (January 6, 2017), http://www.foxnews.com/politics/2017/01/06/intel-report-on-russian-interference-finds-no-documents-forged.html.

[34] Matt Flegenheimer and Scott Shane, "Intelligence Chief Criticizes 'Disparagement' of Findings on Russian Hacking," *The New York Times*, January 5, 2017, http://www.nytimes.com/2017/01/05/us/politics/armed-services-committee-john-mccain-russia-hacking.html.

[35] Mark Hensch, "US caught Russian officials cheering Trump win: report," Text, *TheHill*, (January 5, 2017), http://thehill.com/policy/international/russia/312961-us-caught-russian-officials-cheering-trump-win-report.

[36] "Declassified Report Says Putin 'Ordered' Effort to Undermine Faith in U.S. Election and Help Trump," *Washington Post*, accessed January 7, 2017, https://www.washingtonpost.com/world/national-security/intelligence-chiefs-expected-in-new-york-to-brief-trump-on-russian-hacking/2017/01/06/5f591416-d41a-11e6-9cb0-54ab630851e8_story.html.

[37] "In Trump's Ongoing Feud about Russia, He Says Those Opposed to Better Relations 'Fools,'" Text.Article, *FoxNews.Com*, (January 7, 2017), http://www.foxnews.com/politics/2017/01/07/in-trumps-ongoing-feud-about-russia-says-those-opposed-to-better-relations-fools.html.

[38] Thomas Fernandez, "CNN Has Dossier That Suggests Russia Can Blackmail Trump," *Newstalk Florida*, January 10, 2017, https://www.newstalkflorida.com/featured/cnn-dossier-trump-russia-blackmail/.

[39] "Russia, Trump Deny Report Moscow Has Compromising Info on President-Elect," Text.Article, *FoxNews.Com*, (January 11, 2017), http://www.foxnews.com/politics/2017/01/11/russia-says-it-has-no-compromising-material-on-trump.html.

NOTES

[40] "CNN's Jake Tapper Fires Back at Trump's 'Fake News' Charge - The Daily Beast," accessed January 19, 2017, http://www.thedailybeast.com/articles/2017/01/17/cnn-s-jake-tapper-fires-back-at-trump-s-fake-news-charge.html; David A. Graham, "What CNN's Report on Trump and Russia Does and Doesn't Say," *The Atlantic*, January 10, 2017, https://www.theatlantic.com/politics/archive/2017/01/what-cnns-bombshell-report-does-and-doesnt-say/512747/; "Trump to CNN: 'You Are Fake News,'" *USA TODAY*, accessed May 16, 2017, https://www.usatoday.com/story/news/politics/onpolitics/2017/01/11/trump-cnn-press-conference/96447880/; Evan Perez CNN Jim Sciutto, Jake Tapper and Carl Bernstein, "Intel Chiefs Presented Trump with Claims of Russian Efforts to Compromise Him," *CNN*, accessed May 16, 2017, http://www.cnn.com/2017/01/10/politics/donald-trump-intelligence-report-russia/index.html; Dylan Byers, "BuzzFeed's Publication of Trump Memos Draws Controversy," *CNNMoney*, January 10, 2017, http://money.cnn.com/2017/01/10/media/buzzfeed-trump-report/index.html.

CHAPTER VI

[1] Manu Raju CNN Deirdre Walsh and David Wright, "Trump Asking Congress, Not Mexico, to Pay for Border Wall," *CNN*, accessed January 7, 2017, http://www.cnn.com/2017/01/05/politics/border-wall-house-republicans-donald-trump-taxpayers/index.html; Michael D. Shear and Emmarie Huetteman, "Trump Insists Mexico Will Pay for Wall After U.S. Begins the Work," *The New York Times*, January 6, 2017, http://www.nytimes.com/2017/01/06/us/politics/trump-wall-mexico.html.
[2] "Trump Tells Obama's Ambassadors to Leave by Inauguration Day," Text.Article, *FoxNews.Com*, (January 6, 2017), http://www.foxnews.com/politics/2017/01/06/trump-tells-obamas-ambassadors-to-leave-by-inauguration-day.html.
[3] Jessie Hellmann, "Biden: Trump's Supreme Court nominee deserves hearing and vote," Text, *TheHill*, (January 5, 2017), http://thehill.com/homenews/news/312953-biden-democrats-

124

NOTES

shouldnt-deny-trumps-scotus-nominee-a-hearing-and-a-vote.
[4] Alex Johnson, "In Historic Move, Sen. Cory Booker to Testify against Jeff Sessions," *NBC News*, January 10, 2017, http://www.nbcnews.com/politics/white-house/sen-cory-booker-rep-john-lewis-testify-against-jeff-sessions-n705011; "Donald Trump's 'First Attempt to Ignore the Law,'" *Washington Post*, accessed January 10, 2017, https://www.washingtonpost.com/news/the-fix/wp/2017/01/10/donald-trumps-first-attempt-to-ignore-the-law/.
[5] "Highlights: Trump's Plan to Separate Himself from Business Empire," Text.Article, *FoxNews.Com*, (January 11, 2017), http://www.foxnews.com/politics/2017/01/11/highlights-trumps-plan-to-separate-himself-from-business-empire.html; "Fact-Checking President-Elect Trump's News Conference," *Washington Post*, accessed January 12, 2017, https://www.washingtonpost.com/news/fact-checker/wp/2017/01/11/fact-checking-president-elect-trumps-news-conference/; Jim Rutenberg, "As Trump Berates News Media, a New Strategy Is Needed to Cover Him," *The New York Times*, January 12, 2017, https://www.nytimes.com/2017/01/12/business/media/trump-media-news-conference.html; Arata Yamamoto et al., "'Daring and Crazy Guy': World Weighs in on Donald Trump's Comments," *NBC News*, January 12, 2017, http://www.nbcnews.com/news/world/trump-press-conference-world-reaction-president-elect-s-comments-n706011.
[6] "CNN's Jake Tapper Fires Back at Trump's 'Fake News' Charge - The Daily Beast."
[7] "4 Take-Aways from Rex Tillerson Hearing to Be Secretary of State," *USA TODAY*, accessed January 12, 2017, http://www.usatoday.com/story/news/world/2017/01/11/take-aways-rex-tillerson-hearing-secretary-state/96465338/.
[8] "Defense Secretary Nominee Mattis Warns World Order under Historic Threat," Text.Article, *FoxNews.Com*, (January 12, 2017), http://www.foxnews.com/politics/2017/01/12/mattis-vows-to-strengthen-military-if-confirmed-for-top-pentagon-job.html.

NOTES

[9] "Betsy DeVos, Trump's Education Pick, Lauded as Bold Reformer, Called Unfit for Job," *Washington Post*, accessed January 19, 2017, https://www.washingtonpost.com/local/education/senators-to-scrutinize-betsy-devos-trumps-pick-for-education-secretary/2017/01/17/3a0e6168-da8f-11e6-9a36-1d296534b31e_story.html.

[10] Michael M. Grynbaum, "Trump Team Considers Moving Press Corps, Alarming Reporters," *The New York Times*, January 15, 2017, https://www.nytimes.com/2017/01/15/business/media/trump-white-house-press-corps.html.

[11] "'Fox News Effect' out in Force for Trump, Pew Survey Finds," *USA TODAY*, accessed January 19, 2017, http://www.usatoday.com/story/tech/news/2017/01/18/fox-news-effect-out-force-trump-survey-says/96692432/.

[12] "Trump Gets Facts Wrong in Attacks against NBC's 'Today' Show - Jan. 18, 2017," accessed January 19, 2017, http://money.cnn.com/2017/01/18/media/nbc-today-show-donald-trump-tweets/.

[13] Dave Itzkoff, "Donald Trump News Conference Gets the 'S.N.L.' Treatment," *The New York Times*, January 15, 2017, https://www.nytimes.com/2017/01/15/arts/donald-trump-saturday-night-live.html; "Meryl Streep Takes on Donald Trump at Golden Globes - NBC News," accessed January 10, 2017, http://www.nbcnews.com/pop-culture/awards/meryl-streep-takes-donald-trump-golden-globes-n704571; "Nancy Sinatra Destroys Donald Trump With Her Kickass Tweets | The Huffington Post," accessed January 19, 2017, http://www.huffingtonpost.com/entry/nancy-sinatra-donald-trump-my-way_us_58803a9be4b02c1837e9c2ec.

[14] "Nicole Kidman Says the Country Needs to Get behind President Trump | Fox News," accessed January 12, 2017, http://www.foxnews.com/entertainment/2017/01/12/nicole-kidman-says-country-needs-to-get-behind-president-trump.html.

[15] "Kanye West Visits Donald Trump - The New York Times," accessed December 14, 2016, http://www.nytimes.com/2016/12/13/us/politics/kanye-trump-tower-

NOTES

visit.html?_r=0.

[16] "Linda Bean Calls Anti-Trump Boycotts 'Un-American,' Form of Bullying | Fox Business," accessed January 12, 2017, http://www.foxbusiness.com/features/2017/01/12/linda-bean-calls-anti-trump-boycotts-un-american-form-bullying.html.

[17] "Trump Inauguration Boycott Escalates," *BBC News*, January 18, 2017, sec. US & Canada, http://www.bbc.com/news/world-us-canada-38656271; "President-Elect Trump Attacks Civil Rights Icon Who Said His Presidency Not 'Legitimate' - ABC News," accessed January 19, 2017, http://abcnews.go.com/Politics/president-elect-trump-attacks-civil-rights-icon-presidency/story?id=44777274.

[18] "In Trump Nation, Healing Is Overrated," accessed January 19, 2017, http://www.usatoday.com/story/news/politics/2017/01/17/post-election-political-healing-trump-nation-says-democrats-heal-thyself/96483356/; "With His Choice Of Inauguration Prayer Leaders, Trump Shows His Values," *NPR.Org*, accessed January 19, 2017, http://www.npr.org/2017/01/13/509558608/with-his-choice-of-inauguration-prayer-leaders-trump-shows-his-values.

[19] "First Sign of Enhanced U.S.-Russia Relations under Trump: An Invite to Syria Talks - The Washington Post," accessed January 19, 2017, https://www.washingtonpost.com/world/national-security/first-sign-of-enhanced-us-russia-relations-under-trump-an-invite-to-syria-talks/2017/01/13/81d443d6-d9b9-11e6-9f9f-5cdb4b7f8dd7_story.html?utm_term=.6f90ec970f4c; "Trump Hints at European Immigration Restrictions - CNNPolitics.Com," accessed January 19, 2017, http://www.cnn.com/2017/01/15/politics/donald-trump-europe-immigration-merkel-brexit-interview/; "Trump Worries Nato with 'Obsolete' Comment," *BBC News*, January 16, 2017, sec. US & Canada, http://www.bbc.com/news/world-us-canada-38635181; "Trump's Blast Sends Chill across Europe - CNNPolitics.Com," accessed January 19, 2017, http://www.cnn.com/2017/01/17/politics/donald-trump-nato-europe/; "Trump Vows 'Insurance for Everybody' in Obamacare Replacement Plan," *Washington Post*, accessed January 19, 2017, https://www.washingtonpost.com/politics/trump-vows-insurance-for-everybody-in-obamacare-replacement-plan/2017/01/15/5f2b1e18-

NOTES

db5d-11e6-ad42-f3375f271c9c_story.html.

CHAPTER VII

[1] "Inaugural Address: Trump's Full Speech," *CNN*, accessed February 3, 2017, http://www.cnn.com/2017/01/20/politics/trump-inaugural-address/index.html.
[2] "Trump's Inauguration: How'd He Do?," *CNN*, accessed February 3, 2017, http://www.cnn.com/2017/01/20/opinions/inauguration-opinion-roundup/index.html; "217 Arrests, 6 Officer Injuries during Inauguration Protests," *USA TODAY*, accessed February 3, 2017, http://www.usatoday.com/story/news/politics/2017/01/20/day-protests-arrests-expected-trump-becomes-president/96788208/.
[3] Z. Byron Wolf CNN, "Comparing Trump's Inauguration Crowd to the Women's March," *CNN*, accessed February 3, 2017, http://www.cnn.com/2017/01/21/politics/womens-march-donald-trump-inauguration-sizes/index.html.
[4] A. B. C. News, "More Than 1 Million Rally at Women's Marches in US and Around World," *ABC News*, January 23, 2017, http://abcnews.go.com/Politics/womens-march-heads-washington-day-trumps-inauguration/story?id=44936042.
[5] "Trump Administration Goes To War With The Media Over Inauguration Crowd Size," *NPR.Org*, accessed February 3, 2017, http://www.npr.org/2017/01/21/510994742/trump-administration-goes-to-war-with-the-media-over-inauguration-crowd-size; CNN, "Comparing Trump's Inauguration Crowd to the Women's March."
[6] "Wall Street Ends Higher as Trump Becomes President," *Reuters*, January 21, 2017, http://www.reuters.com/article/us-usa-stocks-idUSKBN1541O1.
[7] "Major U.S. Market Indices Value Over Time - Trailing Year," accessed February 7, 2017, https://w.graphiq.com/w/6RXJauYeR7f?data-width=584&data-height=457&data-href=https%3A%2F%2Fgraphiq.com&data-script-version=true&data-sv=1.1.1&data-index=0.

NOTES

[8] "In Trump We Trust: Inauguration Prompts Celebration in Russia," *Reuters*, January 20, 2017, http://www.reuters.com/article/us-usa-trump-inauguration-russia-idUSKBN1541S6.

[9] "Trump Speaks With Putin In Saturday Phone Call," *NPR.Org*, accessed February 9, 2017, http://www.npr.org/sections/parallels/2017/01/29/512268735/trump-speaks-with-putin-in-50-minute-phone-call.

[10] "Flynn Was Probed by FBI over Calls with Russian Ambassador, Official Says," Text.Article, *FoxNews.Com*, (February 15, 2017), http://www.foxnews.com/politics/2017/02/15/flynn-was-reportedly-probed-by-fbi-over-calls-with-russian-official.html; Howard Kurtz, "Media Helped Force out Flynn, but Leakers' Real Target Is Donald Trump," Text.Article, *FoxNews.Com*, (February 15, 2017), http://www.foxnews.com/politics/2017/02/15/media-helped-force-out-flynn-but-leakers-real-target-is-donald-trump.html.

[11] "Trump Wants a Border Wall but Few in Congress Want to Pay for It," *Los Angeles Times*, accessed April 25, 2017, http://www.latimes.com/politics/washington/la-na-essential-washington-updates-lawmakers-say-flynn-sidestepped-1493134802-htmlstory.html.

[12] AP January 22, 2017, and 7:46 Pm, "Israeli Leader Accepts Invitation from Trump to Visit U.S.," accessed February 6, 2017, http://www.cbsnews.com/news/benjamin-netanyahu-accepts-invitation-from-president-donald-trump-to-visit-us/.

[13] "President Trump Tells Israel to Halt New Settlement Construction," *NY Daily News*, accessed February 9, 2017, http://www.nydailynews.com/news/politics/president-trump-tells-israel-halt-settlement-construction-article-1.2963016.

[14] Gina Mei, "Lawsuit Alleges President Trump Is Violating the Constitution," *Cosmopolitan*, January 23, 2017, http://www.cosmopolitan.com/politics/a8628386/crew-lawsuit-donald-trump-constitution-violation/.

[15] Emily Schultheis CBS News January 22, 2017, and 1:44 Pm, "President Trump Will Not Release His Tax Returns, Adviser Says," accessed February 6, 2017, http://www.cbsnews.com/news/president-trump-will-not-release-his-tax-returns-adviser-says/.

Notes

[16] "Trump Wrongly Blames Fraud for Loss of Popular Vote," *ABC7 Los Angeles*, January 24, 2017, http://abc7.com/1717703/; A. B. C. News, "Trump Still Believes Millions Voted Illegally: White House," *ABC News*, January 25, 2017, http://abcnews.go.com/Politics/trump-believes-voter-fraud-spicer-investigate/story?id=45016322.

[17] "President Trump to Move Forward with Voter Fraud Probe; Set to Sign Executive Order," *FOX6Now.Com*, January 26, 2017, http://fox6now.com/2017/01/26/president-trump-to-move-forward-with-voter-fraud-probe-set-to-sign-executive-order/.

[18] Marina Fang, "Trump Adviser Defends President's Lies On Voter Fraud, Despite Providing No Evidence," *Huffington Post*, February 12, 2017, sec. Politics, http://www.huffingtonpost.com/entry/donald-trump-voter-fraud_us_58a07a9ae4b0ab2d2b15d5e8.

[19] Phil Helsel, "President Trump Signs Executive Order on Obamacare after Swearing-In," *NBC News*, January 21, 2017, http://www.nbcnews.com/storyline/inauguration-2017/trump-signs-executive-action-obamacare-inauguration-day-n710116; Seth Chandler, "President Trump's Day 1 Executive Order Can Severely Damage Obamacare," *Forbes*, accessed February 3, 2017, http://www.forbes.com/sites/theapothecary/2017/01/20/president-trumps-day-1-executive-order-can-severely-damage-obamacare/.

[20] CBS News January 23, 2017, and 12:03 Pm, "Donald Trump Signs Three Executive Memos," accessed February 3, 2017, http://www.cbsnews.com/news/donald-trump-to-sign-executive-orders/.

[21] Matthew Cooper On 1/27/17 at 3:37 PM, "Donald Trump Is the Most Unlikely Anti-Abortion President Ever," *Newsweek*, January 27, 2017, http://www.newsweek.com/trump-unlikely-pro-life-549375.

[22] Peter Baker and Coral Davenport, "Trump Revives Keystone Pipeline Rejected by Obama," *The New York Times*, January 24, 2017, https://www.nytimes.com/2017/01/24/us/politics/keystone-dakota-pipeline-trump.html.

[23] "How President Trump's Pipeline Giveaways Prove He's a Terrible Dealmaker," *Fortune*, accessed February 7, 2017, http://fortune.com/2017/01/25/donald-trump-keystone-pipeline-2/.

NOTES

[24] A. B. C. News, "President Trump Signs Order to 'Dramatically Reduce' Business Regulations," *ABC News*, January 30, 2017, http://abcnews.go.com/Politics/president-trump-orders-limits-business-regulations/story?id=45141440.

CHAPTER VIII

[1] "Will Marco Rubio Defy President Trump on His Pick for Secretary of State?," *Washington Post*, accessed February 6, 2017, https://www.washingtonpost.com/politics/will-marco-rubio-defy-president-trump-on-his-pick-for-secretary-of-state/2017/01/22/433c0968-af0d-4a60-a09f-31ce93724164_story.html.

[2] "President Trump's Education Secretary Nominee Is Dangerously Close to Not Being Confirmed," February 1, 2017, http://theweek.com/speedreads/677501/president-trumps-education-secretary-nominee-dangerously-close-not-being-confirmed.

[3] "Virtually All Senate Democrats Poised to Vote against Remaining Cabinet Picks," *Washington Post*, accessed February 13, 2017, https://www.washingtonpost.com/powerpost/virtually-all-democrats-poised-to-vote-against-remaining-trump-cabinet-picks/2017/02/06/4493bee0-eca9-11e6-9662-6eedf1627882_story.html.

[4] "Trump: Dem Senator Praised Sessions Privately, But Won't Support Him Because of 'Politics,'" Text.Article, *FOX News Insider*, (February 7, 2017), http://insider.foxnews.com/2017/02/07/trump-listening-session-sheriffs-new-sheriff-town-crime-drugs-border-wall.

[5] Azam Ahmed, "As Trump Orders Wall, Mexico's President Considers Canceling U.S. Trip," *The New York Times*, January 25, 2017, https://www.nytimes.com/2017/01/25/world/americas/trump-mexico-border-wall.html; Julie Hirschfeld Davis, "Trump Orders Mexican Border Wall to Be Built and Plans to Block Syrian Refugees," *The New York Times*, January 25, 2017, https://www.nytimes.com/2017/01/25/us/politics/refugees-immigrants-wall-trump.html.

Notes

[6] "Mexico President Cancels U.S. Visit After Trump Wall Comments," Text.Article, *Reuters*, (January 26, 2017), http://www.foxbusiness.com/politics/2017/01/26/mexico-president-cancels-u-s-visit-after-trump-wall-comments.html.

[7] A. B. C. News, "President Trump's Executive Orders on Immigration Explained," *ABC News*, January 27, 2017, http://abcnews.go.com/Politics/president-trumps-executive-orders-immigration-explained/story?id=45062485; Kirk Semple, "Trump and Mexican President Speak by Phone Amid Dispute Over Wall," *The New York Times*, January 27, 2017, https://www.nytimes.com/2017/01/27/world/americas/trump-mexican-president-phone-call.html.

[8] {#pmad-Byline-Frame{width:620px !important; Height:120px !important;}}, "Everything We Know about What Trump Called the 'Worst Deal Ever' between the US and Australia," *Business Insider*, accessed February 13, 2017, http://www.businessinsider.com/what-is-the-us-australia-refugee-deal-trump-immigration-2017-2.

[9] A. B. C. News, "Trump Orders Suspension of All Refugees, Immigrants From Some Muslim Nations," *ABC News*, January 28, 2017, http://abcnews.go.com/Politics/president-trump-signs-executive-actions-pentagon/story?id=45096609.

[10] Michael D. Shear Kulish Nicholas and Alan Feuer, "Judge Blocks Trump Order on Refugees Amid Chaos and Outcry Worldwide," *The New York Times*, January 28, 2017, https://www.nytimes.com/2017/01/28/us/refugees-detained-at-us-airports-prompting-legal-challenges-to-trumps-immigration-order.html; Richard Pérez-peña, "Trump's Immigration Ban Draws Deep Anger and Muted Praise," *The New York Times*, January 28, 2017, https://www.nytimes.com/2017/01/28/us/trumps-immigration-ban-disapproval-applause.html.

[11] "Republicans Begin to Break With President Trump," *Time*, accessed February 9, 2017, http://time.com/4652966/donald-trump-refugee-ban-executive-order-republicans/.

[12] Matt Vespa, "Friendly Reminder: Obama Selected The List Of Muslim Countries in Trump's Executive Order," *Townhall*, accessed February 9, 2017,

NOTES

http://townhall.com/tipsheet/mattvespa/2017/01/29/news-bulletin-the-list-of-muslim-nations-in-trumps-socalled-muslim-ban-are-ones-obama-choose-n2278021.

[13] "Trump Fires Acting AG Sally Yates after She Declines to Defend Travel Ban - CNNPolitics.Com," accessed February 9, 2017, http://www.cnn.com/2017/01/30/politics/donald-trump-immigration-order-department-of-justice/; Sam Stein, "Obama Weighs In On President Trump For The First Time," *Huffington Post*, January 30, 2017, sec. Politics, http://www.huffingtonpost.com/entry/barack-obama-donald-trump-immigration-ban_us_588f8f70e4b0c90efeff0ed0.

[14] Eugene Scott CNN, "Trump on Travel Ban: 'Call It What You Want,'" *CNN*, accessed February 9, 2017, http://www.cnn.com/2017/02/01/politics/donald-trump-ban-bad-people-out/index.html.

[15] "Trump Questions UC Berkeley Funding after Protest," *ABC7 San Francisco*, February 2, 2017, http://abc7news.com/1733468/.

[16] "President Trump Likes to Move Fast. The Public Isn't Thrilled.," *Washington Post*, accessed February 13, 2017, https://www.washingtonpost.com/news/the-fix/wp/2017/02/03/the-trump-administration-is-very-proud-of-how-fast-its-moving-the-public-is-less-thrilled/.

[17] Matthew Dessem and Matthew Dessem, "Saturday Night Live Gives America What It Wants: Leslie Jones Playing Trump, Who Is Still President," *Slate*, February 12, 2017, http://www.slate.com/blogs/browbeat/2017/02/12/leslie_jones_plays_donald_trump_who_is_still_president.html.

[18] Richard Pérez-peña, "In Libel Suit, Melania Trump Cites Loss of Chance to Make Millions," *The New York Times*, February 7, 2017, https://www.nytimes.com/2017/02/07/us/politics/melania-trump-libel-suit-daily-mail.html; The New York Times, "Melania Trump and Daily Mail Settle Her Libel Suits," *The New York Times*, April 12, 2017, https://www.nytimes.com/2017/04/12/business/media/melania-trump-daily-mail-libel.html.

NOTES

[19] Richard Pérez-peña and Rachel Abrams, "Trump Assails Nordstrom for 'Unfairly' Dropping His Daughter Ivanka's Line," *The New York Times*, February 8, 2017, https://www.nytimes.com/2017/02/08/business/ivanka-trump-nordstrom-tj-maxx.html.

[20] "White House Rebuffs Ethics Office Recommendation to Discipline Kellyanne Conway," *Washington Post*, accessed March 2, 2017, https://www.washingtonpost.com/news/post-politics/wp/2017/03/01/white-house-rebuffs-ethics-office-recommendation-to-discipline-kellyanne-conway/.

[21] "'I Don't Believe in Fake News': MSNBC Host Says She Will No Longer Book Kellyanne Conway on Show," *TheBlaze*, February 15, 2017, http://www.theblaze.com/news/2017/02/15/i-dont-believe-in-fake-news-msnbc-host-says-she-will-no-longer-book-kellyanne-conway-on-show/.

[22] "President Donald Trump Poised to Reveal His Selection for Supreme Court Early This Week," *FOX6Now.Com*, January 30, 2017, http://fox6now.com/2017/01/29/president-donald-trump-poised-to-reveal-his-selection-for-supreme-court-early-this-week/.

[23] "Congressional Democrats Close Ranks Against Trump," *Time*, accessed February 9, 2017, http://time.com/4654574/donald-trump-congress-democrats-reaction/.

[24] "President Trump Nominates Neil Gorsuch To The Supreme Court," *NPR.Org*, accessed February 9, 2017, http://www.npr.org/2017/01/31/512708127/president-trump-to-announce-supreme-court-nominee-shortly.

[25] "President Trump To Senate Leader: 'Go Nuclear' To Confirm Gorsuch," *NPR.Org*, accessed February 9, 2017, http://www.npr.org/2017/02/01/512872512/president-trump-to-senate-leader-go-nuclear.

[26] Jon Russell, "Federal Judge Puts Nationwide Block on President Trump's Travel Ban," *TechCrunch*, accessed February 9, 2017, http://social.techcrunch.com/2017/02/03/federal-judge-puts-nationwide-block-on-president-trumps-travel-ban/.

NOTES

[27] Kevin Liptak Producer CNN White House, "Trump Just Got Checked and Balanced," *CNN*, accessed February 13, 2017, http://www.cnn.com/2017/02/04/politics/donald-trump-travel-ban/index.html.

[28] "Appeal Filed to Overturn Halt of President Trump's Travel Ban," *Whotv.Com*, February 5, 2017, http://whotv.com/2017/02/04/appeal-filed-to-overturn-halt-of-president-trumps-travel-ban/; "Court Denies Trump Request to Immediately Restore Travel Ban," *ABC7 Chicago*, February 5, 2017, http://abc7chicago.com/1738506/.

[29] "Trump's Blasts at Judge Raise Questions for Gorsuch on Independence - Chicago Tribune," accessed February 13, 2017, http://www.chicagotribune.com/news/nationworld/politics/ct-trump-judge-gorsuch-20170205-story.html.

[30] "The White House Is Really Splitting Hairs on Neil Gorsuch's Rebuke of President Trump," *Washington Post*, accessed February 13, 2017, https://www.washingtonpost.com/news/the-fix/wp/2017/02/09/president-trump-is-in-denial-about-his-own-supreme-court-justice-rebuking-him/.

[31] Carolyn Tyler, "Judges Focus on Whether Trump's Order Is Muslim Ban," *ABC7 San Francisco*, February 7, 2017, http://abc7news.com/1742370/; Steve Almasy and Darran Simon CNN, "Timeline: How President Trump's Travel Ban Unraveled," *CNN*, accessed February 13, 2017, http://www.cnn.com/2017/02/10/us/trump-travel-ban-timeline/index.html.

[32] "'We'Ll Win That Battle': Trump Could File New Travel Executive Order on Monday," Text.Article, *FOX News Insider*, (February 10, 2017), http://insider.foxnews.com/2017/02/10/president-trump-could-file-new-travel-immigration-executive-order-monday; A. B. C. News, "President Trump Continues Twitter Attack on Courts over Stay of Immigration Order," *ABC News*, February 12, 2017, http://abcnews.go.com/Politics/president-trump-continues-twitter-attack-courts-stay-immigration/story?id=45437662.

NOTES

[33] "Trump Kicks Executive Order Back to 9th District Judges," *LifeZette*, February 13, 2017, http://www.lifezette.com/polizette/trump-kicks-executive-orders-back-9th-district-judges/.
[34] "Defense Secretary Mattis Issues New Ultimatum to NATO Allies on Defense Spending," *Washington Post*, accessed February 16, 2017, https://www.washingtonpost.com/news/checkpoint/wp/2017/02/15/mattis-trumps-defense-secretary-issues-ultimatum-to-nato-allies-on-defense-spending/.
[35] "Trump Names Alexander Acosta as New Pick for Labor Secretary," *Washington Post*, accessed February 16, 2017, https://www.washingtonpost.com/news/get-there/wp/2017/02/16/trump-to-name-alexander-acosta-as-new-pick-for-labor-secretary/.
[36] "Senate Confirms Rep. Mick Mulvaney as Trump's Budget Chief," *Washington Post*, accessed February 16, 2017, https://www.washingtonpost.com/news/wonk/wp/2017/02/16/senators-confirm-trumps-pick-to-deal-with-the-federal-budget/.
[37] "Senate Votes to Confirm Former Texas Governor Rick Perry as Energy Secretary," *Washington Post*, accessed March 2, 2017, https://www.washingtonpost.com/news/energy-environment/wp/2017/03/02/senate-votes-to-confirm-former-texas-governor-rick-perry-as-energy-secretary/.

CHAPTER IX

[1] Cyra Master, "Trump blasts 'out of control' media dishonesty," Text, *TheHill*, (February 16, 2017), http://thehill.com/homenews/administration/319914-trump-blasts-out-of-control-media-dishonesty.
[2] "Analysis | Donald Trump Delivers a Series of Raw and Personal Attacks on the Media in a News Conference for the Ages," *Washington Post*, accessed February 16, 2017, https://www.washingtonpost.com/news/the-fix/wp/2017/02/16/donald-trump-delivers-a-series-of-raw-and-wild-

NOTES

attacks-on-the-media-in-a-press-conference-for-the-ages/.
[3] "President Trump Speaks to Supporters 'Without the Filter of the Fake News,'" Text.Article, *FOX News Insider*, (February 18, 2017), http://insider.foxnews.com/2017/02/18/donald-trump-campaign-rally-melbourne-florida.
[4] "Trump Supporters See a Successful President — and Are Frustrated with Critics Who Don't," *Washington Post*, accessed February 28, 2017, https://www.washingtonpost.com/politics/trump-supporters-see-a-successful-president--and-are-frustrated-with-critics-who-dont/2017/02/19/496cb4b4-f6ca-11e6-9845-576c69081518_story.html.
[5] "Trump Will Be First President In 36 Years To Skip White House Correspondents' Dinner," *NPR.Org*, accessed March 1, 2017, http://www.npr.org/2017/02/25/517257273/trump-will-be-first-president-in-36-years-to-skip-white-house-correspondents-din.
[6] "Analysis | Fact-Checking President Trump's CPAC Speech," *Washington Post*, accessed March 1, 2017, https://www.washingtonpost.com/news/fact-checker/wp/2017/02/24/fact-checking-president-trumps-cpac-speech/.
[7] Sewell Chan, "'Last Night in Sweden'? Trump's Remark Baffles a Nation," *The New York Times*, February 19, 2017, https://www.nytimes.com/2017/02/19/world/europe/last-night-in-sweden-trumps-remark-baffles-a-nation.html.
[8] Farhad Manjoo, "I Ignored Trump News for a Week. Here's What I Learned.," *The New York Times*, February 22, 2017, https://www.nytimes.com/2017/02/22/technology/trump-news-media-ignore.html.
[9] "Perspective | President Trump Wants to Put on a Show. Governing Matters Less.," *Washington Post*, accessed March 1, 2017, https://www.washingtonpost.com/posteverything/wp/2017/02/24/president-trump-wants-to-put-on-a-show-governing-matters-less/.
[10] "The Latest: Trump Intends to Donate Salary, Spokesman Says," *Washington Post*, accessed March 13, 2017, https://www.washingtonpost.com/politics/federal_government/the-latest-trump-compares-health-care-bill-to-obama-ratings/2017/03/13/b3454290-0807-11e7-bd19-

NOTES

fd3afa0f7e2a_story.html.

[11] Steven Bertoni, "Billionaire Tom Steyer Talks About His Plan To Fight President Trump," *Forbes*, accessed March 1, 2017, http://www.forbes.com/sites/stevenbertoni/2017/02/22/billionaire-tom-steyer-talks-about-his-plan-to-fight-president-trump/.

[12] Matthew Rozsa, "Michael Moore Launches Website Devoted to Stopping President Trump," *Salon*, accessed March 1, 2017, http://www.salon.com/2017/02/21/michael-moore-launches-website-devoted-to-stopping-president-trump/.

[13] "George Clooney Slams President Trump, Steve Bannon," Text.Article, *FoxNews.Com*, (February 22, 2017), http://www.foxnews.com/entertainment/2017/02/22/george-clooney-slams-president-trump-steve-bannon.html.

[14] "President Trump: Budget Proposal Will Focus on Spending Cuts," *FOX6Now.Com*, February 23, 2017, http://fox6now.com/2017/02/22/president-trump-budget-proposal-will-focus-on-spending-cuts/.

[15] Glenn Thrush Kelly Kate and Maggie Haberman, "Trump to Ask for Sharp Increases in Military Spending, Officials Say," *The New York Times*, February 26, 2017, https://www.nytimes.com/2017/02/26/us/politics/trump-budget.html; Rafi Letzter, 7h, and 329 1, "Trump's Budget Could Cut 3,000 Staff from the EPA, Report Suggests," *Business Insider*, accessed March 2, 2017, http://www.businessinsider.com/trump-budget-epa-lay-off-2017-3.

[16] Robert Pear and Kate Kelly, "Trump Concedes Health Law Overhaul Is 'Unbelievably Complex,'" *The New York Times*, February 27, 2017, https://www.nytimes.com/2017/02/27/us/politics/trump-concedes-health-law-overhaul-is-unbelievably-complex.html.

[17] Jeremy W. Peters Becker Jo and Julie Hirschfeld Davis, "Trump Rescinds Rules on Bathrooms for Transgender Students," *The New York Times*, February 22, 2017, https://www.nytimes.com/2017/02/22/us/politics/devos-sessions-transgender-students-rights.html.

NOTES

[18] The Editorial Board, "President Trump Takes Aim at the Environment," *The New York Times*, February 23, 2017, https://www.nytimes.com/2017/02/23/opinion/president-trump-takes-aim-at-the-environment.html.
[19] "Holder: Obama Preparing to Get Back into Political Spotlight," Text.Article, *FoxNews.Com*, (March 2, 2017), http://www.foxnews.com/politics/2017/03/02/holder-obama-preparing-to-get-back-into-political-spotlight.html; "The Latest."
[20] "Analysis | Fact-Checking President Trump's CPAC Speech."
[21] A. B. C. News, "President Trump, First Lady Host First Ball at White House," *ABC News*, February 27, 2017, http://abcnews.go.com/Politics/president-trump-lady-host-governors-dinner-white-house/story?id=45753442.
[22] "Trump Will Be First President In 36 Years To Skip White House Correspondents' Dinner."
[23] Julie Hirschfeld Davis Shear Michael D. and Peter Baker, "Trump, in Optimistic Address, Asks Congress to End 'Trivial Fights,'" *The New York Times*, February 28, 2017, https://www.nytimes.com/2017/02/28/us/politics/trump-address-congress.html.
[24] "Analysis | Fact-Checking President Trump's Address to Congress," *Washington Post*, accessed March 1, 2017, https://www.washingtonpost.com/news/fact-checker/wp/2017/02/28/fact-checking-president-trumps-address-to-congress/.
[25] "Calling For 'Renewal Of The American Spirit,' Trump Outlines His Vision," *NPR.Org*, accessed March 1, 2017, http://www.npr.org/2017/02/28/517826209/watch-live-president-trump-looks-for-reset-with-joint-address-to-congress.
[26] Karen Yourish and Paul Murray, "The Highs and Lows of President Trump's Job Approval," *The New York Times*, February 28, 2017, https://www.nytimes.com/interactive/2017/02/28/us/politics/the-highs-and-lows-of-trumps-approval.html.
[27] Peter Baker, "Former President George W. Bush Levels Tacit Criticism at Trump," *The New York Times*, February 27, 2017, https://www.nytimes.com/2017/02/27/us/politics/george-w-bush-

NOTES

criticism-trump.html.

[28] "Dow Busts through 21,000 Threshold on Feel-Good Trump Message," *Washington Post*, accessed March 2, 2017, https://www.washingtonpost.com/business/economy/dow-busts-through-21000-threshold-on-feel-good-trump-message/2017/03/01/ed7688f2-feb1-11e6-99b4-9e613afeb09f_story.html.

[29] Evan Perez CNN Shimon Prokupecz and Eli Watkins, "Sessions Did Not Disclose Meetings with Russian Ambassador," *CNN*, accessed March 2, 2017, http://www.cnn.com/2017/03/01/politics/jeff-sessions-russian-ambassador-meetings/index.html; Michael D. Shear and Charlie Savage, "Trump Has 'Total' Confidence in Sessions; Lawmakers Seek Recusal," *The New York Times*, March 2, 2017, https://www.nytimes.com/2017/03/02/us/politics/jeff-sessions-russia-trump-investigation-democrats.html.

[30] Matthew Rosenberg Goldman Adam and Michael S. Schmidt, "Obama Administration Rushed to Preserve Intelligence of Russian Election Hacking," *The New York Times*, March 1, 2017, https://www.nytimes.com/2017/03/01/us/politics/obama-trump-russia-election-hacking.html.

[31] "Putin Aide: Clinton Advisers Met with Russian Ambassador 'Lots' of Times," Text.Article, *Washington Examiner*, (March 13, 2017), http://www.foxnews.com/politics/2017/03/13/putin-aide-clinton-advisers-met-with-russian-ambassador-lots-times.html.

[32] Brooke Seipel, "Report: Trump furious that Sessions recused himself," Text, *TheHill*, (March 4, 2017), http://thehill.com/blogs/blog-briefing-room/news/322363-reports-trump-told-aides-sessions-shouldnt-have-recused-himself; "Attorney General Jeff Sessions Will Recuse Himself from Any Probe Related to 2016 Presidential Campaign," *Washington Post*, accessed March 6, 2017, https://www.washingtonpost.com/powerpost/top-gop-lawmaker-calls-on-sessions-to-recuse-himself-from-russia-investigation/2017/03/02/148c07ac-ff46-11e6-8ebe-6e0dbe4f2bca_story.html.

NOTES

[33] Tim Lister CNN, "Russia on Trump: From Glee to Frustration," *CNN*, accessed March 6, 2017, http://www.cnn.com/2017/03/06/europe/trump-russia-lister/index.html; Angela Dewan and Kara Fox CNN, "Trump and Russia: What the Fallout Could Be," *CNN*, accessed March 6, 2017, http://www.cnn.com/2017/03/05/politics/trump-russia-fallout/index.html.

[34] Jeff Zeleny and Kevin Liptak CNN, "Obama Irked and Exasperated in Response to Trump's Wiretapping Claims, Sources Say," *CNN*, accessed March 9, 2017, http://www.cnn.com/2017/03/08/politics/donald-trump-barack-obama-wiretapping/index.html; Tom LoBianco CNN, "GOP Hill Leaders Back Away from Trump on Wiretap Allegations," *CNN*, accessed March 9, 2017, http://www.cnn.com/2017/03/07/politics/wiretap-congress-sean-spicer-response/index.html; Michael S. Schmidt, "White House Rejects Comey's Assertion That Wiretapping Claim Is False," *The New York Times*, March 6, 2017, https://www.nytimes.com/2017/03/06/us/politics/trump-rejects-comeys-assertion-that-wiretapping-claim-is-false-spokeswoman-says.html.

CHAPTER X

[1] "Revised Executive Order Bans Travelers from Six Muslim-Majority Countries from Getting New Visas," *Washington Post*, accessed March 6, 2017, https://www.washingtonpost.com/world/national-security/new-executive-order-bans-travelers-from-six-muslim-majority-countries-applying-for-visas/2017/03/06/3012a42a-0277-11e7-ad5b-d22680e18d10_story.html.

[2] "Federal Judge to Hear First Lawsuit against New Travel Ban - CNNPolitics.Com," accessed March 9, 2017, http://www.cnn.com/2017/03/07/politics/hawaii-travel-ban-lawsuit/.

Notes

[3] Alexander Burns, "2 Federal Judges Rule Against Trump's Latest Travel Ban," *The New York Times*, March 15, 2017, https://www.nytimes.com/2017/03/15/us/politics/trump-travel-ban.html; Laura Jarrett, "Federal Judge Sides with Trump Administration in Travel Ban Case," *CNN*, accessed March 30, 2017, http://www.cnn.com/2017/03/24/politics/virginia-federal-judge-revised-travel-ban/index.html.

[4] "The Daily 202: Trump Will Use Bully Pulpit to Counter Conservative Revolt over Obamacare Replacement," *Washington Post*, accessed March 8, 2017, https://www.washingtonpost.com/news/powerpost/paloma/daily-202/2017/03/08/daily-202-trump-will-use-bully-pulpit-to-counter-conservative-revolt-over-obamacare-replacement/58bfb74ee9b69b1406c75d4d/; "GOP ObamaCare Repeal Plan Forges Ahead, amid Mounting Resistance," Text.Article, *FoxNews.Com*, (March 8, 2017), http://www.foxnews.com/politics/2017/03/08/gop-leaders-forge-ahead-on-obamacare-overhaul-amid-mounting-resistance.html; Mike Debonis, "Conservatives Lash out at House GOP's Obamacare Replacement Bill," *BlabberBuzz*, accessed March 8, 2017, https://blabber.buzz/politics/progressive/112260-conservatives-lash-out-at-house-gops-obamacare-replacement-bill.

[5] Maggie Haberman, "Trump Tells Planned Parenthood Its Funding Can Stay If Abortion Goes," *The New York Times*, March 6, 2017, https://www.nytimes.com/2017/03/06/us/politics/planned-parenthood.html.

[6] Stephen Collinson CNN, "CBO Score Gives Obamacare Repeal Biggest Test Yet," *CNN*, accessed March 16, 2017, http://www.cnn.com/2017/03/13/politics/cbo-report-republican-health-care/index.html.

[7] "24 Million Would Lose Health Insurance Coverage under GOP's Obamacare Replacement by 2026," accessed March 16, 2017, http://www.cnbc.com/2017/03/13/cbo-says-millions-lose-health-insurance-under-gop-obamacare-replacement.html; Dan Mangan, "Trump Says 'I Know' Clinton Voters Would Do Better than His Voters under GOP's Health Plan," *CNBC*, March 16, 2017,

NOTES

http://www.cnbc.com/2017/03/16/trump-i-know-clinton-voters-would-do-better-under-obamacare-repeal.html; Jennifer Steinhauer and Thomas Kaplan, "G.O.P. Senators Suggest Changes for Health Care Bill Offered by House," *The New York Times*, March 14, 2017, https://www.nytimes.com/2017/03/14/us/politics/paul-ryan-healthcare.html.

[8] Julie Hirschfeld Davis Kaplan Thomas and Robert Pear, "Trump Warns House Republicans: Repeal Health Law or Lose Your Seats," *The New York Times*, March 21, 2017, https://www.nytimes.com/2017/03/21/us/politics/house-republicans-health-care-donald-trump.html; MJ Lee CNN Lauren Fox and Eli Watkins, "Trump May Move GOP Health Care Bill to the Right," *CNN*, accessed March 23, 2017, http://www.cnn.com/2017/03/19/politics/trump-health-care-senate/index.html; "GOP Leaders Delay ObamaCare Replacement Vote, amid Opposition," Text.Article, *FoxNews.Com*, (March 23, 2017), http://www.foxnews.com/politics/2017/03/23/gop-leaders-scramble-to-get-lawmakers-behind-obamacare-replacement.html.

[9] Daniel Arkin, "House Lawmakers Ask DOJ to Offer Wiretapping Evidence by Monday," *NBC News*, March 13, 2017, http://www.nbcnews.com/politics/donald-trump/house-intelligence-panel-wants-wiretapping-evidence-monday-n732451.

[10] Manu Raju CNN Tom LoBianco and Ashley Killough, "Republicans Lose Patience with FBI on Russia, Trump Campaign Ties Information," *CNN*, accessed March 16, 2017, http://www.cnn.com/2017/03/14/politics/wiretapping-congressional-investigation/index.html.

[11] Eli Lake, "Trump's Wiretap Claims Are Bogus. But He's Still Onto Something.," *Bloomberg View*, March 15, 2017, https://www.bloomberg.com/view/articles/2017-03-15/trump-s-wiretap-claims-are-bogus-but-he-s-still-onto-something.

[12] "Nunes: No Evidence of Trump Tower Wiretapping," *US News & World Report*, accessed March 16, 2017, https://www.usnews.com/news/politics/articles/2017-03-15/devin-nunes-no-evidence-to-back-donald-trumps-wiretapping-claims.

Notes

[13] "Analysis | The White House Serves up a Red Herring on Russia," *Washington Post*, accessed March 23, 2017, https://www.washingtonpost.com/news/the-fix/wp/2017/03/20/the-white-house-serves-up-a-red-herring-on-russia/; Sean Hannity, "Comey's FBI Can Only Comment If It Hurts President Trump," Text.Article, *FoxNews.Com*, (March 21, 2017), http://www.foxnews.com/opinion/2017/03/21/sean-hannity-james-comeys-fbi-cant-comment-unless-it-hurts-president-trump.html.

[14] Euan McKirdy CNN, "White House: Trump Will Attend NATO Leaders Meeting in May," *CNN*, accessed March 23, 2017, http://www.cnn.com/2017/03/22/politics/trump-nato-leaders-meeting/index.html.

[15] "LOOK: Climate Change Protesters Carve Message on Trump Golf Course Green," Text.Article, *FOX News Insider*, (March 13, 2017), http://insider.foxnews.com/2017/03/13/trump-golf-course-vandalized-california-climate-change-protesters.

[16] Mary Papenfuss, "Donald Trump's Approval Rating Is In The Toilet," *Huffington Post*, March 20, 2017, sec. Politics, http://www.huffingtonpost.com/entry/trump-approval-rating_us_58cf74b7e4b0be71dcf5b696; Eugene Scott CNN, "WSJ Editorial: Most Americans May Conclude Trump 'Fake President,'" *CNN*, accessed March 23, 2017, http://www.cnn.com/2017/03/22/politics/donald-trump-wsj-trust/index.html; "Artist Defends Anti-Trump Billboard," Text.Article, *FoxNews.Com*, (March 20, 2017), http://www.foxnews.com/us/2017/03/20/artist-defends-anti-trump-billboard.html.

[17] A. O. L. Staff, "Poll Shows Americans Trust 3 Media Outlets More than Trump," *AOL.Com*, accessed March 30, 2017, https://www.aol.com/article/news/2017/03/30/poll-shows-americans-trust-some-media-outlets-more-than-trump/22018350/.

[18] Cody Derespina, "Trump Hits MSNBC for 'FAKE NEWS' after Tax Return Report," Text.Article, *Fox News*, (March 15, 2017), http://www.foxnews.com/politics/2017/03/15/trump-hits-msnbc-for-fake-news-after-tax-return-report.html; "Five Things to Know about Trump's Leaked Tax Return," *POLITICO*, accessed March 16, 2017,

NOTES

http://politi.co/2mtzZsj.

[19] "Ivanka Trump's Move To The White House Raises Questions About Ethics," *NPR.Org*, accessed March 23, 2017, http://www.npr.org/sections/thetwo-way/2017/03/21/520965076/ivanka-trumps-move-to-the-white-house-raises-questions-about-ethics.

[20] Dan Merica CNN Gloria Borger, Jim Acosta and Betsy Klein, "Ivanka Trump Is Making Her White House Job Official," *CNN*, accessed March 30, 2017, http://www.cnn.com/2017/03/29/politics/ivanka-trump-white-house-job/index.html.

[21] Brian Stelter, "In Interview about His Falsehoods, President Trump Offers New Ones," *CNNMoney*, March 23, 2017, http://money.cnn.com/2017/03/23/media/time-magazine-donald-trump-interview-falsehoods/index.html; "In 'Apprentice' Defamation Case, Trump Will Argue He Is Immune from Lawsuits in State Courts until He Leaves Office," *Washington Post*, accessed March 30, 2017, https://www.washingtonpost.com/news/post-politics/wp/2017/03/28/in-apprentice-defamation-case-trump-will-argue-he-is-immune-from-lawsuits-in-state-courts-until-he-leaves-office/.

[22] Peter Baker Haberman Maggie and Glenn Thrush, "Trump Removes Stephen Bannon From National Security Council Post," *The New York Times*, April 5, 2017, https://www.nytimes.com/2017/04/05/us/politics/national-security-council-stephen-bannon.html.

[23] Jodi Kantor, "For Kushner, Israel Policy May Be Shaped by the Personal," *The New York Times*, February 11, 2017, https://www.nytimes.com/2017/02/11/us/politics/jared-kushner-israel.html.

[24] "Gorsuch Enters High-Stakes Confirmation Hearing after Intensive Preparation," Text.Article, *FoxNews.Com*, (March 20, 2017), http://www.foxnews.com/politics/2017/03/20/gorsuch-enters-high-stakes-confirmation-hearing-after-intensive-preparation.html; Matt Flegenheimer Hulse Adam Liptak, Carl and Charlie Savage, "Seven Highlights From the Gorsuch Confirmation Hearings," *The New York*

NOTES

Times, March 21, 2017, https://www.nytimes.com/2017/03/21/us/politics/neil-gorsuch-confirmation-hearings.html; "Gorsuch Hearings Day 3: Feinstein Presses Judge on Abortion, Physician-Assisted Suicide," *Washington Post*, accessed March 22, 2017, https://www.washingtonpost.com/powerpost/neil-gorsuch-confirmation-hearings-supreme-court-nominee-heads-into-day-3/2017/03/21/2c346a8c-0e93-11e7-ab07-07d9f521f6b5_story.html.
[25] "Schumer Plans for 'Nuclear' Showdown with McConnell," Text.Article, *FoxNews.Com*, (March 24, 2017), http://www.foxnews.com/politics/2017/03/24/schumer-plans-for-nuclear-showdown-with-mcconnell.html.

CHAPTER XI

[1] "GOP Health-Care Bill: House Republican Leaders Abruptly Pull Their Rewrite of the Nation's Health-Care Law," *Washington Post*, accessed March 30, 2017, https://www.washingtonpost.com/powerpost/house-leaders-prepare-to-vote-friday-on-health-care-reform/2017/03/24/736f1cd6-1081-11e7-9d5a-a83e627dc120_story.html; Caroline Linton CBS News March 24, 2017, and 5:25 Pm, "Trump Blames Democrats for House GOP Failure to Pass Health Care Bill," accessed March 30, 2017, http://www.cbsnews.com/news/trump-says-both-parties-can-do-better-after-health-care-bill-pulled/; "Trump Still Optimistic on Health Care Vote, Spicer Says | Fox News," accessed March 30, 2017, http://www.foxnews.com/politics/2017/03/24/house-set-to-vote-on-obamacare-replacement-bill-after-trump-ultimatum.html.
[2] Joseph Weber, "Shutdown Threat Returns after ObamaCare Repeal Meltdown," Text.Article, *FoxNews.Com*, (March 28, 2017), http://www.foxnews.com/politics/2017/03/28/shutdown-threat-returns-after-obamacare-meltdown.html; A. B. C. News, "Trump Takes Aim at Freedom Caucus Again," *ABC News*, March 30, 2017, http://abcnews.go.com/Politics/donald-trump-takes-aim-freedom-caucus-2018-threat/story?id=46464771; Joseph Weber, "Trump vs. Freedom Caucus: President Takes Names, Starting with Amash,"

NOTES

Text.Article, *FoxNews.Com*, (April 1, 2017), http://www.foxnews.com/politics/2017/04/01/trump-vs-freedom-caucus-president-takes-names-starting-with-amash.html.
[3] Coral Davenport and Alissa J. Rubin, "Trump Signs Executive Order Unwinding Obama Climate Policies," *The New York Times*, March 28, 2017, https://www.nytimes.com/2017/03/28/climate/trump-executive-order-climate-change.html.
[4] Adam Housley, "Susan Rice Requested to Unmask Names of Trump Transition Officials, Sources Say," Text.Article, *FoxNews.Com*, (April 3, 2017), http://www.foxnews.com/politics/2017/04/03/susan-rice-requested-to-unmask-names-trump-transition-officials-sources-say.html; https://www.facebook.com/nakamuradavid, "Trump's White House Struggles to Get out from under Russia Controversy," *Washington Post*, accessed April 12, 2017, https://www.washingtonpost.com/politics/trumps-white-house-struggles-to-get-out-from-under-russia-controversy/2017/03/31/89c3f470-1626-11e7-ada0-1489b735b3a3_story.html.
[5] Miranda Green and Manu Raju CNN, "FBI Monitored Former Trump Campaign Adviser Carter Page on Russia," *CNN*, accessed April 12, 2017, http://www.cnn.com/2017/04/12/politics/fbi-carter-page-russia/index.html.
[6] Joseph Weber, "Carter Page: Media, 'Corrupt Clinton Regime' Kept Tying Me to Trump Team," Text.Article, *FoxNews.Com*, (April 23, 2017), http://www.foxnews.com/politics/2017/04/23/carter-page-media-corrupt-clinton-regime-kept-tying-me-to-trump-team.html.
[7] Chad Pergram, "What Is the Nuclear Option? Roadmap to How Gorsuch Confirmation Could Play Out," Text.Article, *FoxNews.Com*, (April 3, 2017), http://www.foxnews.com/politics/2017/04/03/what-is-nuclear-option-roadmap-to-how-gorsuch-confirmation-could-play-out.html; Judson Berger, "Republicans Go 'Nuclear,' Bust through Democratic Filibuster on Gorsuch," Text.Article, *FoxNews.Com*, (April 6, 2017), http://www.foxnews.com/politics/2017/04/06/senate-republicans-tee-up-nuclear-showdown-on-gorsuch.html; Douglas Schoen, "Five Important Takeaways from the Gorsuch Nomination

NOTES

Fight," Text.Article, *FoxNews.Com*, (April 10, 2017), http://www.foxnews.com/opinion/2017/04/10/five-important-takeaways-from-gorsuch-nomination-fight.html.

[8] "Tillerson Says Coalition Forming to Target Assad, Trump Hearing Military Options," Text.Article, *FoxNews.Com*, (April 6, 2017), http://www.foxnews.com/politics/2017/04/06/tillerson-says-coalition-forming-to-target-assad-trump-hearing-military-options.html.

[9] CNN, "White House Sending Mixed Signals on Syria Ahead of G7 Summit," *WCPO*, April 10, 2017, http://www.wcpo.com/news/national/white-house-sending-mixed-signals-on-syria-ahead-of-g7-summit; "White House Accuses Russia of Syria Chemical Attack 'Cover Up,'" *Reuters*, April 12, 2017, http://www.reuters.com/article/us-g7-foreign-syria-idUSKBN17D0GI.

[10] Ryan Gaydos, "China's Xi Tells Trump He Wants Peaceful Solution to North Korea," Text.Article, *FoxNews.Com*, (April 12, 2017), http://www.foxnews.com/politics/2017/04/12/chinas-xi-tells-trump-wants-peaceful-solution-to-north-korea.html.

[11] Gerry Mullany Buckley Chris and David E. Sanger, "China Warns of 'Storm Clouds Gathering' in U.S.-North Korea Standoff," *The New York Times*, April 14, 2017, https://www.nytimes.com/2017/04/14/world/asia/north-korea-china-nuclear.html; A. B. C. News, "Amid North Korea Crisis, Pence Becomes Trump Emissary Abroad," *ABC News*, April 24, 2017, http://abcnews.go.com/International/wireStory/amid-north-korea-crisis-pence-trump-emissary-abroad-46965062; "Trump Discusses North Korea Tensions with Asian Leaders," Text.Article, *Fox News*, (April 24, 2017), http://www.foxnews.com/politics/2017/04/24/trump-discusses-north-korea-tensions-with-asian-leaders.html; Edmund DeMarche, "Full Senate Heads to Rare Classified Meeting at the White House on North Korea," Text.Article, *Fox News*, (April 26, 2017), http://www.foxnews.com/politics/2017/04/26/full-senate-heads-to-rare-classified-meeting-at-white-house-on-north-korea.html.

NOTES

[12] Alan Rappeport, "Trump's Directive Will Lift Hiring Freeze, as It Asks Agencies for Cuts," *The New York Times*, April 11, 2017, https://www.nytimes.com/2017/04/11/us/politics/trumps-directive-will-lift-hiring-freeze-as-it-asks-agencies-for-cuts.html.
[13] "Trump 100 Days: President Adds Tax Reform in Key Week," Text.Article, *FoxNews.Com*, (April 23, 2017), http://www.foxnews.com/politics/2017/04/23/trump-100-days-president-adds-tax-reform-in-key-week.html.
[14] "White House Demands Disrupt Shutdown Negotiations," *POLITICO*, accessed April 25, 2017, http://politi.co/2pJp1Ez.
[15] "Trump Signals He Is Willing to Drop Demands That Could Spur a Shutdown," *NBC News*, April 25, 2017, http://www.nbcnews.com/politics/congress/congress-scrambling-fund-government-ahead-friday-deadline-n750401; https://www.facebook.com/amber.j.phillps, "Analysis | The First Brick Hasn't Been Set, and Trump's Border Wall Is Already Going South on Him," *Washington Post*, accessed April 25, 2017, https://www.washingtonpost.com/news/the-fix/wp/2017/04/24/4-reasons-trumps-border-wall-is-already-going-south-on-him/.
[16] Alex Seitz-Wald, "Tax Day Protests to Demand Trump's Returns," *NBC News*, April 14, 2017, http://www.nbcnews.com/storyline/democrats-vs-trump/tax-day-protests-demand-trump-s-returns-n746146; "Trump 100 Days"; https://www.facebook.com/max.ehrenfreund, "Trump Wants to Give the Rich a Big Tax Cut. Here's What His Supporters Want.," *Washington Post*, accessed April 24, 2017, https://www.washingtonpost.com/news/wonk/wp/2017/04/14/trump-wants-to-give-the-rich-a-big-tax-cut-heres-what-his-supporters-want/; CBS/AP April 15, 2017, and 5:14 Pm, "13 Arrested as Violence Breaks out at Dueling Trump Protests in Berkeley," accessed April 25, 2017, http://www.cbsnews.com/news/protesters-arrested-as-pro-trump-and-anti-trump-rallies-clash-in-berkeley/; https://www.facebook.com/steven.mufson, "Trump to Propose Large Increase in Deductions Americans Can Claim on Their Taxes," *Washington Post*, accessed April 26, 2017, https://www.washingtonpost.com/business/economy/washington-

NOTES

braces-for-details-of-trumps-tax-reform-plan/2017/04/25/1fba8b30-29df-11e7-a616-d7c8a68c1a66_story.html.
[17] Seitz-Wald, "Tax Day Protests to Demand Trump's Returns"; "Trump 100 Days"; https://www.facebook.com/max.ehrenfreund, "Trump Wants to Give the Rich a Big Tax Cut. Here's What His Supporters Want."; 15, 2017, and Pm, "13 Arrested as Violence Breaks out at Dueling Trump Protests in Berkeley."
[18] Barnini Chakraborty, "Trump Signs Order to Clamp down on Visa Program, Enforce 'Buy American' Policy," Text.Article, *FoxNews.Com*, (April 18, 2017), http://www.foxnews.com/politics/2017/04/18/trump-signs-order-to-clamp-down-on-foreign-bidders-enforce-buy-american-policy.html.
[19] Cody Derespina, "Trump Slams Sanctuary City Ruling, Says Opponents Are 'Judge Shopping!,'" Text.Article, *Fox News*, (April 26, 2017), http://www.foxnews.com/politics/2017/04/26/trump-slams-sanctuary-city-ruling-says-opponents-are-judge-shopping.html; Vivian Yee, "Judge Blocks Trump Effort to Withhold Money From Sanctuary Cities," *The New York Times*, April 25, 2017, https://www.nytimes.com/2017/04/25/us/judge-blocks-trump-sanctuary-cities.html.
[20] "Trump 100 Days."

CHAPTER XII

[1] https://www.facebook.com/danbalzwapo, "Nearing 100 Days, Trump's Approval at Record Lows but His Base Is Holding," *Washington Post*, 100, accessed April 25, 2017, https://www.washingtonpost.com/politics/nearing-100-days-trumps-approval-at-record-lows-but-his-base-is-holding/2017/04/22/a513a466-26b4-11e7-b503-9d616bd5a305_story.html.
[2] https://www.facebook.com/leadership.washingtonpost, "Analysis | A Short History of Presidents' Complicated Relationship with the 100-Day Milestone," *Washington Post*, accessed April 25, 2017, https://www.washingtonpost.com/news/on-leadership/wp/2017/04/24/a-short-history-of-presidents-complicated-

NOTES

relationship-with-the-100-day-milestone/.
[3] Becket Adams, "It's White House Correspondents' Dinner Time: Why Aren't Media at the Table?," *Washington Examiner*, accessed April 25, 2017, http://www.washingtonexaminer.com/its-white-house-correspondents-dinner-time-why-arent-media-at-the-table/article/2620668.
[4] "Trump Will Keep List of White House Visitors Secret," *Washington Post*, accessed April 25, 2017, https://www.washingtonpost.com/news/post-politics/wp/2017/04/14/trump-to-discontinue-obama-policy-of-voluntarily-releasing-white-house-visitor-logs/.
[5] "Trump: North Korea's Failed Missile Launch 'Disrespected' China," Text.Article, *Fox News*, (April 29, 2017), http://www.foxnews.com/politics/2017/04/29/trump-north-koreas-failed-missile-launch-disrespected-china.html; "Trump Praises China's Xi over Handling of North Korea," *BBC News*, April 28, 2017, sec. Asia, http://www.bbc.com/news/world-asia-39741671.
[6] Kevin Liptak and Dan Merica CNN, "Trump Agrees 'Not to Terminate NAFTA at This Time,'" *CNN*, accessed May 1, 2017, http://www.cnn.com/2017/04/26/politics/trump-nafta/index.html.
[7] Michael D. Shear, "Trump Tells N.R.A. Convention, 'I Am Going to Come Through for You,'" *The New York Times*, April 28, 2017, https://www.nytimes.com/2017/04/28/us/politics/donald-trump-nra.html.
[8] Matt Stevens, "Senator Responds to Trump's N.R.A. Speech With Photos of Shooting Victims," *The New York Times*, April 28, 2017, https://www.nytimes.com/2017/04/28/us/politics/christopher-murphy-guns-trump.html.
[9] "Congress Settles for Stopgap to Avoid Government Shutdown," *Washington Post*, accessed May 2, 2017, https://www.washingtonpost.com/politics/federal_government/senate-dems-block-quick-vote-on-short-term-spending-bill/2017/04/27/1a18f642-2ba8-11e7-9081-f5405f56d3e4_story.html.
[10] Brooke Singman, "Trump Has His Cabinet, but Lagging behind on Other Appointments," Text.Article, *Fox News*, (April 28, 2017), http://www.foxnews.com/politics/2017/04/28/trump-has-his-cabinet-

NOTES

but-lagging-behind-on-other-appointments.html; Nelson D. Schwartz, "G.D.P. Report Shows U.S. Economy Off to Slow Start in 2017," *The New York Times*, April 28, 2017, https://www.nytimes.com/2017/04/28/business/economy/economy-gross-domestic-product-first-quarter.html; https://www.facebook.com/anaclaireswanson and https://www.facebook.com/max.ehrenfreund, "Trump Really Needs an Economic Boom. So Far, He's Not Getting One.," *Washington Post*, accessed May 2, 2017, https://www.washingtonpost.com/news/wonk/wp/2017/04/28/trump-really-needs-an-economic-boom-so-far-hes-not-getting-one/.

[11] https://www.facebook.com/danbalzwapo, "Perspective | Trump Governs as He Campaigned: Unconventionally and Unpredictably," *Washington Post*, accessed May 2, 2017, https://www.washingtonpost.com/politics/at-100-days-trump-governs-as-he-campaigned/2017/04/27/f26708bc-2abe-11e7-a616-d7c8a68c1a66_story.html.

[12] Cody Derespina, "100 Days of Disruption: How Trump Rewrote the Presidential Script," Text.Article, *Fox News*, (April 29, 2017), http://www.foxnews.com/politics/2017/04/29/100-days-disruption-how-trump-rewrote-presidential-script.html.

[13] "(4) GIGANTIC & MASSIVE RALLY: President Donald Trump 100 DAYS RALLY in Harrisburg, Pennsylvania 4/29/17 - YouTube," accessed May 1, 2017, https://www.youtube.com/; "Host Blasts Absent Trump at White House Correspondents' Dinner," *MSN*, accessed May 2, 2017, https://www.msn.com/en-ca/news/politics/host-blasts-absent-trump-at-white-house-correspondents-dinner/ar-BBAyslu; "Donald Trump Attacks US Media at 100-Day Pennsylvania Rally," *BBC News*, April 30, 2017, sec. US & Canada, http://www.bbc.com/news/world-us-canada-39760283.

[14] Peter Baker, "How Trump Has Reshaped the Presidency, and How It's Changed Him, Too," *The New York Times*, April 29, 2017, https://www.nytimes.com/2017/04/29/us/politics/trump-presidency-100-days.html.

NOTES

[15] Ibid.; "Thousands March In D.C. To Protest Trump Climate Policies," *NPR.Org*, accessed May 2, 2017, http://www.npr.org/2017/04/30/526250791/thousands-march-in-d-c-to-protest-trump-climate-policies; Samuel Chamberlain, "'Hardly a Success': Top Dem Schumer Rips Trump over First 100 Days," Text.Article, *Fox News*, (April 30, 2017), http://www.foxnews.com/politics/2017/04/30/hardly-success-top-dem-schumer-rips-trump-over-first-100-days.html.

www.ingramcontent.com/pod-product-compliance
Lightning Source LLC
Chambersburg PA
CBHW032055090426
42744CB00005B/220